MUSCLE CAR

FORD, CHEVY & CHRYSLER

ICONS

MUSCLE CAR

FORD, CHEVY & CHRYSLER
ICONS

MIKE MUELLER

CRESTLINE

CRESTLINE

An imprint of MBI Publishing Company

First published in 2003 by Crestline, an imprint of
MBI Publishing Company, Galtier Plaza, Suite 200,
380 Jackson Street, St. Paul, MN 55101-3885 USA

First published by MBI Publishing Company.

Motorbooks International titles are also available at discounts
in bulk quantity for industrial or sales-promotional use. For
details write to Special Sales Manager at Motorbooks
International Wholesalers & Distributors, Galtier Plaza, Suite
200, 380 Jackson Street, St. Paul, MN 55101-3885 USA.

ISBN 0-7603-1773-9

Front cover: A revised accent stripe up front represented
the most noticeable Camaro SS change for 1968. In 1968,
SS 396 Camaro buyers could choose from three big-block
V-8s, as the 325 horsepower and 375 horsepower 396s
were joined by a 350 horsepower version.

Front banner (left to right): As standard equipment
under an SS 454 Chevelle's bulging hood, the LS5 454
was rated at 365 horsepower. In full-sized applications,
Chevy's LS5 carried the Corvette's 390 horsepower
output rating.

Ford built the legendary Boss 429 Mustang to homologate
the big Boss 429 V-8 for NASCAR competition under
mid-sized model hoods. Under NASCAR rules, a stock
engine was legal as long as it was installed in at least
500 models sold to the public.

Somewhat of a mystery still today, the 1969 COPO 9562
Chevelle was a little-known variation on the big-block
A-body theme. Like the COPO Camaros, this Chevelle
was equipped with the L72 427 Corvette V-8.

A restyled, curvaceous body also graced Dodge's 1971
Charger, a Coke-bottle-shaped creation that rolled on a
wheelbase two inches shorter than previous editions.

On the title page: Helping set the hotter 1970 'Cuda
models apart from their sedate Barracuda and Gran
Coupe brethren were standard fog lights below the
bumper and a sport hood with twin scoops.

On the back cover: When first introduced in 1965,
Shelby American's GT350 Mustang variant was a
single-purpose machine available in one color only,
without a back seat or an automatic transmission,
and loaded with a full collection of standard
race-ready hardware.

CONTENTS

FORD MUSCLE CARS

CHEVY MUSCLE CARS

DODGE/PLYMOUTH MUSCLE CARS

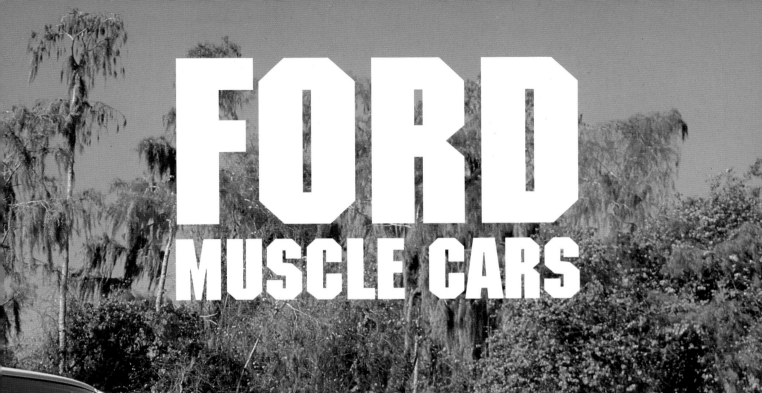

FORD
MUSCLE CARS

Those Super Torque Ford engines climb hills like a homesick Swiss yodeler. One is available with 425 horsepower (a few more than the average private plane). Try <u>total performance</u> on your local Matterhorn.

—Ford advertisement, 1963

Acknowledgments

Special thanks go to all the men and women who allowed their performance Fords to be photographed for this book. In order of appearance, they are:

Charlie and Pam Plylar, Kissimmee, Florida: '71 429 Cobra Jet Mach 1 Mustang; Donald Farr, Lakeland, Florida: '66 Mustang GT; George Baumann, Davie, Florida: '67 Mercury Cougar XR-7 GT; Chris and Deborah Teeling, Enfield, Connecticut: '68-1/2 428 Cobra Jet Mustang; Carl Beck, Clearwater, Florida: '69 428 Cobra Jet Mercury Cougar Eliminator; Barry Larkins, Daytona Beach, Florida: '70 Boss 429 Mustang; Kurt and Connie Heber, Melbourne, Florida: '70 Boss 302 Mustang; Marc Troy, Jr., Latrobe, Pennsylvania: '64 Fairlane Thunderbolt (clone); Jerry and Carol Buczkowski, Mishawaka, Indiana: '66 427 Fairlane; Eddie Kirkland, Lakeland, Florida: '67 Fairlane GT; Jerry Sieradzki, South Bend, Indiana: '67 Mercury 427 Cyclone; Bob Kurtz, East Greenville, Pennsylvania: '69 Fairlane Cobra; Dan Andrews, Lakeland, Florida: '69 Talladega; Hubert and Sandi Miller, Melbourne, Florida: '60 Starliner; Luke and Sue Kirkland, Lakeland, Florida: '63 427 Galaxie; Bill and Barbara Jacobsen, Silver Dollar Classic Cars, Odessa, Florida: '64 427 Galaxie; Robert Schultz, Champaign, Illinois: '66 7-Litre convertible; Rick and Vicki Sattler, St. Petersburg, Florida: '67 7-Litre hardtop; Bill and Barbara Jacobsen, Silver Dollar Classic Cars, Odessa, Florida: '69 Galaxie XL GT 429 and '63 M-code Thunderbird Sports Roadster; Ed and Diann Kuziel, Tampa, Florida: '57 Thunderbird; Jeff Leggate, Savannah, Georgia: '65 Sunbeam Tiger; Dale Nichols, Orlando, Florida: 289 and 427 Cobras; Dave Robb, Titusville, Florida: '67 Shelby GT350 and '67 Shelby GT500.

Introduction

Total Performance

Ford's performance history actually began with a major step backwards. In February 1957, ultra-conservative general manager Robert McNamara agreed to an Automobile Manufacturers Association decree that Detroit's automakers cease all factory racing involvement, discontinue performance parts production, and refrain from using speed teasers in advertisements. Basically a clever ploy by General Motors head Harlow "Red" Curtice, the so-called AMA "ban" on factory performance left Ford Motor Company in the dust as Curtice's GM divisions continued competing in the horsepower race while McNamara focused his attentions on mundane pursuits, like the new, compact Falcon.

In November 1960, thirty-six year old Lee Iacocca stepped in as McNamara moved up. Recognizing that young, performance-minded buyers represented a growing force in the market, Iacocca reacted rapidly to reverse Ford's declining fortunes. Ford officials had already informed GM's front office in April 1959 of plans to offer performance options despite the AMA ban. The result was the 360hp 352ci Police Interceptor V-8, a powerplant that transformed the sleek '60 Starliner coupe into what may best be described as Ford's first muscle car. Progenitor of a long line of hot, big-block, FE-series V-8s, Ford's 352 Police Interceptor was followed by a

Opposite page
Not all Ford muscle cars wore galloping horses or striking cobras. The R-code 425hp 427-equipped Fairlane (left) and W-code 410hp 427 Cyclone (right) were built on intermediate-sized chassis with an eye cast toward drag strip and NASCAR competition. From 1963–67, Ford offered both versions of the 427—the R-code featuring twin four-barrels, the W-code using one four-barrel—although the '66 427 Fairlane used only the twin-carb variety. When four hood pins are pulled, the 427 Fairlane's fiberglass hood simply lifts off.

procession of bigger and better power sources with displacements growing to 390ci in 1961, 406ci in 1962, 427ci in 1963, and 428ci in 1966.

In June 1962, Henry Ford II officially announced his company would no longer comply with the 1957 AMA edict, claiming that "We feel we can better establish our own standards of conduct with respect to the manner in which the performance of our vehicles is to be promoted and advertised." The following April, Iacocca introduced his "Total Performance" campaign. "We at Ford believe in performance," he told the press, "because the search for performance—Total Performance—made the automobile the wonderfully efficient, pleasurable machine it is today—and will make it better tomorrow." And with that, the race was on.

In 1963 and 1964, full-sized Fords powered by the famed 427ci FE V-8 were both boulevard brutes and racing champions. Then came the mass-market miracle called Mustang. Introduced in April 1964, Iacocca's baby created a new breed aptly named "pony car." Originally offering only small-block power, with the 271hp High-Performance 289 representing the top performance option, the Mustang was redesigned for 1967 to make room for the big-block FEs. And in April 1968, the 335hp 428ci Cobra Jet V-8 transformed Ford's pony cars into true street killers.

The next year, Ford made the 428 Cobra Jet standard in a mid-sized body, creating the Fairlane Cobra, a no-nonsense performance machine intended to compete with Plymouth's Road Runner. On the flip side of the coin, 1969 also marked the introduction of the stylish Mach 1 Mustang, a car that offered every bit as much pizzazz as performance. And at the head of the pony car herd were three racing-inspired models: the Trans Am-tested Boss 302; its Mercury cousin, the Cougar Eliminator; and the big-block brute Boss 429 Mustang.

For 1970, Ford debuted a new big-block, the 385-series 429ci Thunder Jet, an engine that offered Torino Cobra buyers 360hp as standard equipment. Like its 428ci counterpart in the Mustang ranks, the '70 Torino Cobra's 429 could also be equipped with Cobra Jet equipment, upping the power ante to 375hp. Returning for a farewell appearance in 1971, the 429 Cobra Jet represented Ford's last great muscle car powerplant as the curtain came down on Dearborn performance. By 1972, strict emissions standards and hefty insurance costs spelled the end for the big-block Cobra Jets, leaving the small-block 351 Cleveland V-8 to carry the Blue Oval banner into the seventies. And when Iacocca replaced the third-generation Mustang with the little Mustang II in 1974, it was made painfully clear that a new age had dawned.

First appearing on full-sized fenders early in 1963, this emblem represented Ford Motor Company's hottest underhood offering until the famed 428 Cobra Jet emerged early in 1968. In 1966, the 427ci FE-series big-block V-8 made its debut in intermediate ranks within Fairlane sheet metal, followed by Mercury's 427 Cyclone in '67. The 427 was last offered in detuned, single-carb, 390hp form in 1968. Few were sold, and the majority of those were included as part of Mercury's GT-E Cougar package.

Chapter 1

Wild Horses

Ford's Mustang Kicked off a New Breed

On April 17, 1964, Ford Motor Company unleashed a sales blitz the likes of which Detroit had never seen, rushing the Mustang to market after first teasing the press with a small, two-seat sports car prototype in 1962. Commonly credited in full to Lee Iacocca, Ford's phenomenal pony car was instant front-page news, making simultaneous appearances on the covers of both *Time* and *Newsweek*. Dealers were swamped with orders for the affordable sportster with the long hood, bucket seats, and floor shifter. Within twelve months, the Mustang had broken Ford's own record for first-year sales established by the utilitarian Falcon in 1960. After twenty-four months, total pony car production had surpassed one million.

For most buyers, Ford's Mustang offered economical, practical transportation with a sporty flair. Standard power originally came from a feeble 170ci six-cylinder, with optional 260ci and 289ci Windsor V-8s waiting in the wings. Anxious to harness the new pony car performance image, Ford engineers introduced the truly hot 271hp "K-code" High-Performance 289 in June 1964. Following in August was a sporty "2+2" fastback body style joining the hardtop and convertible models. Then in April 1965, Ford debuted the GT equipment group to help mark the Mustang's one-year anniversary. Featuring various suspension upgrades and appearance items, the GT package represented the top of the heap in pony car performance for 1965 and '66.

Opposite page
What a difference five years can make. In 1966, Ford's first-generation Mustang (right) was a relatively nimble, sporty compact armed only with a Windsor small-block in top performance trim. By 1971, the third-generation Mustang had grown into anything but a compact and could be ordered with Dearborn's largest, most powerful V-8, the 429 Cobra Jet, rated at 370hp.

GT exterior features included fog lamps and a special grille bar, twin exhaust trumpets exiting through the rear valance panel, a lower body stripe, "GT" fender identification, and these optional knock-off wheel covers. Attractive, 14in, styled steel wheels were also available.

But then came the competition's response. GM debuted its own pony cars in 1967, Chevrolet's Camaro and Pontiac's Firebird, both featuring optional big-block V-8s. Also new for '67 was Mercury's Cougar, a longer, more luxurious version of its Mustang cousin. To stay in the race, Ford Motor Company offered the venerable 390ci FE-series big-block V-8 as an option for both the Cougar and Mustang, a move that required enlarging the '67 Mustang body, an idea with which Iacocca wholeheartedly disagreed. Even with big-block power, however, Dearborn's pony cars were quickly left behind by high-powered rivals, a situation that was rectified with a vengeance the following year.

In April 1968, Ford introduced the 428 Cobra Jet Mustang, a super-stock drag car for the street that Hot Rod's Eric Dahlquist called "the fastest regular production sedan ever built." On the street, the new Cobra Jet Mustangs were easy 14sec performers; at the track, they were NHRA Winternational champions—either way, Ford had a real winner.

Complementing the Cobra Jet's optional 335hp in 1969 was the new Mach 1 Sports-Roof Mustang offering loads of sporty looks, some nice luxury touches, and ample beef underneath. New as well for '69 were the Boss 302 and Boss 429 Mustangs, the former built to homologate a hot, small-block pony car for Trans Am competition, the latter doing the same for its NASCAR-inspired engine only. Mercury's Cougar Eliminator was also introduced in '69 with Trans Am competition in mind, although it was available with a full range of optional FoMoCo power sources ranging from the high-winding Boss 302 small-block to the stump-pulling 428 Cobra Jet big-block.

The 428 CJ returned for one last year as a Mustang option in 1970. Meanwhile, the 351 Cleveland small-block was debuting as the Boss 429 was being phased out. Featuring free-breathing, Boss 302-type canted-valve heads, the hot 300hp 351 Cleveland was offered as standard equipment under '70 Cougar Eliminator hoods. Both the Eliminator and Boss 302 Mustang would follow the Boss 429 by year's end.

Big news for 1971 was a radically larger Mustang body and an optional 429ci 385-

To celebrate the Mustang's first birthday, Ford introduced two attractive options packages in April 1965: the interior decor group—often called the "pony interior" for its "running horses" seat inserts—and the GT equipment group. Available only with 289ci four-barrel V-8s, the 225hp version or the 271hp "Hi Po," the GT option group included various appearance pieces along with some serious performance hardware. Front disc brakes were included, as was a special handling package that featured heavier springs, stiffer shocks, quicker 22:1 steering, and a larger front stabilizer bar. Inside, a five-dial instrument cluster was added.

Mercury's Cougar debuted in 1967 on a stretched Mustang platform with simulated leather buckets, hideaway headlights, and V-8 power all as standard equipment. Amply impressed, *Motor Trend*'s editors named it their "Car of the Year." Like Ford's Mustang, Mercury's top performance Cougar featured the GT package, a $323 option that included power front discs, a performance handling package, Firestone Wide Oval rubber, and the 320hp 390ci big-block V-8. According to *Car and Driver*, a '67 Cougar GT could run 0–60mph in 6.5sec. This GT is also an XR-7 model, a fully loaded Cougar option package introduced in February 1967. XR-7 features included a wood-rimmed steering wheel, black-face competition-type instrumentation in a simulated walnut dash, toggle switches, an overhead console, a leather-covered T-handle automatic transmission shifter, and combination leather/vinyl seats.

series V-8 in place of the 428 CJ. Available with or without ram air, and in Cobra Jet and Super Cobra Jet form, the 429 CJ was rated at 370hp regardless of accompanying equipment. And with the Boss 302 and Boss 429 gone, Ford rolled out its Boss 351 Mustang for '71, perhaps as a farewell to pony car performance. Powered by a High Output 300hp 351 Cleveland, the Boss 351 was a high-13sec screamer, as well as a suitable send-off for the Mustang performance bloodline. Once the big 429s were gone after '71, only the Cleveland small-blocks were around to carry on, and that legacy ended as well with the Mustang II's arrival in 1974.

Having fallen behind the pony car performance crowd, Ford made an impressive comeback in 1968, introducing the 428 Cobra Jet Mustang on April 1. Available as fastbacks, hardtops, or convertibles, all Cobra Jet Mustangs were GT models, meaning they were equipped with heavy-duty suspension, styled steel wheels wearing F70 rubber, fog lamps, body side C-stripes, "GT" fender emblems, and quad exhaust tips. Additional standard Cobra Jet Mustang features included a functional Ram-Air hood with distinctive black striping, front disc brakes, and a heavy-duty 9in rearend.

This '68-1/2 Cobra Jet Mustang still wears its Tasca Ford dealer emblem. Tasca Ford, located in East Providence, Rhode Island, was a mecca for Ford performance fans in the sixties, and it was Bob Tasca who actually inspired Ford to build the Cobra Jet Mustang. Not satisfied with the 390ci-equipped Mustang, Tasca's men built their own "King of the Road" prototype in 1967 using various FE-series V-8 components. Tasca then demonstrated his KR Mustang in Dearborn, leading to Ford's decision to build the 428 Cobra Jet.

Left
Inside, four-speed Cobra Jet Mustangs were equipped with an 8000rpm tach as standard; tachs were optional when the C6 automatic transmission was chosen. Four-speed Cobra Jets also received staggered rear shocks, while all 428 CJ Mustangs came with braced shock towers up front. Bottom line was about $3,600, roughly $1,000 more than a base 2+2 '68 Mustang. According to *Hot Rod*, a specially prepared Cobra Jet Mustang prototype roared through the quarter-mile in 13.56sec at 106.64mph. Actual quarter-mile performance for a typical Cobra Jet was probably in the low 14sec range.

Ford engineers based the Cobra Jet V-8 on a 428ci passenger car block. On top went 427 low-riser heads, a cast-iron copy of the aluminum Police Interceptor intake manifold, and a 735cfm Holley four-barrel carburetor.

A 390 GT cam, PI connecting rods, and 10.6:1 pistons completed the package. Advertised output was 335hp, a conservative figure that fooled very few.

Mercury's Cougar Eliminator first appeared in prototype form at the Los Angeles Auto Show in October 1968. The model created enough of a stir to justify regular production, and the official introduction came in April 1969. Everything about the car was eye-popping, from its radiant paint schemes and large hood scoop, to its front and rear spoilers. Competition suspension, including heavy springs and shocks and a large front sway bar, was standard, with a rear sway bar optionally available.

Eliminator color choices numbered five—blue, orange, yellow, gold, and green—all of them glaring. External identification on 1969 models included a bodyside stripe that terminated in "Eliminator" lettering just behind the door; for '70, the stripe ran the length of the car and the lettering was moved to the lower rear quarters. Production of Eliminators in '69 was 2,411 and 2,200 in 1970.

Standard Eliminator power in 1969 came from a 290hp 351 Windsor small-block V-8. Available at extra cost was a 320hp 390ci FE, the 290hp Boss 302 canted-valve small-block, and this 335hp 428 Cobra Jet big-block. In a *Super Stock & Drag Illustrated* magazine test, a '69 428 CJ Cougar ran the quarter-mile in 13.91sec, topping out at 103.9mph.

Standard Eliminator equipment included F70x14in Goodyear Polyglas rubber on styled steel wheels with blank center caps. Eliminators equipped with the optional 428 Cobra Jet V-8, like this one, also received higher rate springs, an even thicker front sway bar, and staggered rear shocks.

The Cobra Jet will be the utter delight of every Ford lover and the bane of all the rest because, quite frankly, it is the fastest running Pure Stock in the history of man.

—*Hot Rod*, March 1968

Previous pages
Ford built the legendary Boss 429 Mustang to homologate the big Boss 429 V-8 for NASCAR competition under mid-sized model hoods. Under NASCAR rules, a stock engine was legal as long as it was installed in at least 500 models sold to the public. Since the specific model used wasn't important, Dearborn officials decided to install the Boss 429 in pony car sheet metal. Partially assembled '69 and '70 Mustang SportsRoofs were sent to the Kar Kraft works in Brighton, Michigan, where all Boss 429 modifications were made. A front chin spoiler and large, functional hood scoop were standard on the Boss 429. Hood scoops on '69 models were painted body color, while '70 Boss 429s used a black scoop.

Modifications required to fit the Boss 429 into the Mustang's engine bay included moving the spring towers one inch farther apart. To help compensate for the new nose-heavy stance, the front A-arms were also lowered one inch. Among chassis features were front disc brakes, Gabriel shocks, and a rear stabilizer bar. Boss 429 Mustangs also received fender decal identification, dual color-keyed racing mirrors, and 15in Magnum 500 wheels. An engine oil cooler under the hood and a trunk-mounted battery were part of the package as well.

Featuring aluminum "semi-hemi" heads with staggered valves, Ford's Boss 429 V-8 could breathe with the best of them—so well, in fact, that the standard 735cfm Holley four-barrel couldn't keep up with the big engine's appetite. Advertised output was 375hp and 450lb-ft of torque. While the first 279 '69 Boss 429s had magnesium valve covers, remaining '69s and all '70s wore these aluminum covers. Known as

NASCAR versions, the first 279 Boss 429 engines used hydraulic cams and 1/2in connecting rod bolts and can be identified by their "820 S" engine tag code. The other 580 '69 models and most '70 Boss 429s received the 820 T engine with a mechanical cam and 3/8in rod bolts. Extremely rare is the 820 A Boss 429 which featured minor modifications to the Thermactor smog equipment.

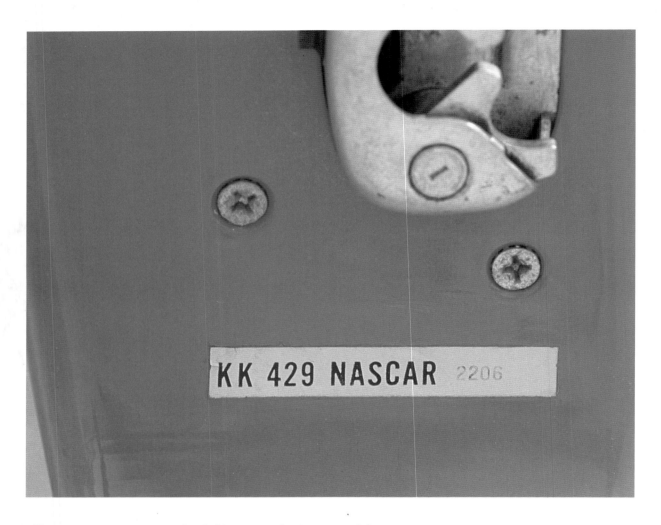

KK 429 NASCAR 2206

All Boss 429 Mustangs received this Kar Kraft production number sticker on the driver's door denoting the cars' status as NASCAR homologation models. Production of Boss 429s in Brighton spanned but twelve months beginning in January 1969, with '70 models first rolling down the line that September. KK production numbers for 1969 Boss 429s ran from 1201 to 2059 as total production reached 859. This Grabber Blue '70 Boss 429 is one of 499 built; accordingly, '70 model KK numbers ran from 2060 to 2558

Right
Lowering the Boss 429, widening its track, and using big F60 Goodyear rubber on 15in Magnum 500 wheels required some custom modification to the front fender wheel openings to allow clearance. Kar Kraft's people obtained ample clearance by rolling in the wheel opening lip.

Ford president Semon "Bunkie"Knudsen, a performance-minded manager with a background in GM projects like the Z/28 Camaro, simply demanded that Ford build "absolutely the best-handling street car available on the American market." The result was the Boss 302 Mustang, first offered in 1969, and again in '70. Chassis engineer Matt Donner met Knudsen's demand with fat F60 rubber on 15in wheels, competition springs, a stiff front sway bar, and staggered heavy-duty shocks in back. After driving a '69 Boss 302, *Car and Driver*'s staff called it "the best handling Ford ever to come out of Dearborn and [it] just may be the new standard by which everything from Detroit must be judged." Designer Larry Shinoda, a former GM employee probably best known for his work on the '63 Corvette Sting Ray, supplied the Boss 302's exterior appeal with graphics, spoilers, and slats. A front chin spoiler, black-striped hood, "Boss 302" bodyside stripes that draped over the cowl, dual color-keyed racing mirrors, and blacked-out rear deck and cove panel were all standard. Optional dress-up items included rear window slats and a rear deck wing. Thanks to the big 15in, 60-series tires, Boss 302s had their front fender lips rolled in similar fashion to Boss 429 front fenders. Magnum 500 wheels were optional.

Left
With free-breathing, canted-valve Cleveland heads equipped with big valves (2.23in intake, 1.71in exhaust), the Boss 302 could wind like nobody's business, up to 7000rpm by factory claims, which is why a rev limiter was included in the package. A 780cfm Holley carburetor on an aluminum intake delivered fuel/air to the combustion chambers with the help of a .477in lift, 290-degree duration solid-lifter cam. Compression was 10.5:1. In 1970, intake valve size decreased to 2.19in and chrome valve covers were replaced by aluminum units. Maximum output for the Boss 302 was advertised as 290hp at 5800rpm.

A name was chosen: Mustang, to honor the legendary high-performance World War II fighter— though the misconception that it meant the horse didn't hurt; either was as American as apple pie and both suggested fast movement.

—Randy Leffingwell,
American Muscle

Above left
All Boss 302 Mustangs in 1969 and '70 came equipped with this Autolite rev limiter mounted on the engine compartment wall just ahead of the driver's side shock tower. If not disconnected or removed by the owner—a common occurrence—this limiter restricted the high-winding Boss small-block to 6150rpm.

A total restyle in 1971 transformed the Mustang into "a fat pig" in Iacocca's terms, but a bigger body built around Ford's biggest engines was what Bunkie Knudsen had wanted during his short Dearborn tenure. In keeping with tradition, the '71 Mach 1 featured a host of performance imagery and heavy-duty hardware. A black honeycomb grille with rectangular "sportslamps," color-keyed urethane front bumper, dual racing mirrors, black or argent (depending on exterior color) lower body paint, special body side stripe, blacked out rear cove, chrome exhaust extensions, and appropriate "Mach1 Mustang" fender and rear deck decals were all standard. Optional dress-up included a front chin spoiler, Magnum 500 wheels, and rear wing spoiler. Standard 14in wheels featured flat hubcaps and trim rings. Although complaints about its girth and poor rearward visibility were many, most felt the '71 Mach 1 was an attractive machine. As *Sports Car Graphic* explained, "whatever [the car] isn't, it is exciting, and . . . no Mach 1 is going to rust in a showroom."

Left
Standard power for the '71 Mach 1 was a 302ci two-barrel small-block, but if real muscle was the aim, the only choice was the optional 429 Cobra Jet, available with an optional ram air hood and/or the Drag Pack equipment which then transformed it into a Super Cobra Jet. Beefier internals, an external oil cooler, and a choice between a 3.91:1 Traction-Lok or 4.30:1 Detroit Locker rearend were just a few of the Super Cobra Jet's features. With or without ram air, Cobra Jet or Super Cobra Jet, the performance 429s were advertised by Ford at 370hp in 1971. At the track, that power translated into a 13.97sec 100mph quarter-mile run according to *Super Stock* magazine.

The blacked-out treatment and tie-down pins were standard Mach 1 fare in 1971, but the NACA-ducted hood was an option with the base 302ci small-block. Although ordering a 351 or 429 automatically included the NACA hood, the twin scoops weren't functional unless the optional ram air equipment was ordered as well.

Chapter 2

Mid-Sized Maulers

Thunderbolts, Cyclones, and Cobras

Named after Henry Ford's estate, Ford's Fairlane nameplate first appeared on Dearborn's flagships in 1955. Replaced at the top by the Galaxie lineup in 1959, the Fairlane moniker was last used in the full-sized ranks in 1961, but reappeared the following year. "Some cars have new names," read factory brochures, "this name has a new car." Introduced for 1962, the new intermediate Fairlane was nearly one foot shorter than the big Galaxie, yet was eight inches longer than the compact Falcon. Also introduced that year was an innovative, lightweight V-8 created through a technique known as thin-wall casting. Initially displacing 221ci, the Fairlane V-8 was 90lb lighter and considerably more compact than the popular Chevrolet small-block V-8.

Early performance enhancements included the mid-year 1962 "Lively Ones" promotion, when Ford Motor Company rolled out the Fairlane 500 Sports Coupe. Included in the Sports Coupe deal were bucket seats and a mini-console. Also available at extra cost was the 260 Challenger V-8, a bored-out version of the 221. In 1963, engineers again punched out displacement mid-year, resulting in the 289 Challenger V-8, a reasonably hot small-block that delivered 271hp in optional "High-Performance" trim.

Big news in 1964 involved two new offerings, one for the street and one for the

Opposite page
Introduced in the spring of 1966 as yet another ploy to legalize a high-performance package for super-stock drag racing, Ford's second 427 Fairlane wasn't quite as radical as the '64 Thunderbolt, yet was a still a force to be reckoned with. Built as no-nonsense racing machines, all were Wimbledon White Fairlane 500 hardtops (no XLs or GTs) armed with the 425hp, dual-carb 427ci medium-riser V-8. Standard equipment included front disc brakes and a fiberglass scooped hood held down by pins at all four corners.

Homologating a specific performance model for NHRA super-stock drag racing in 1964 required a production run of at least fifty units; Ford ended up building twice that many Thunderbolts, which ran as A/FX (factory experimental) competitors until the first fifty were completed. To save weight, these racing Fairlanes were equipped with various fiberglass components, including the distinctive teardrop-scooped hood (required to clear the 427 High Riser's dual carburetors), fenders, and front bumpers (some later Thunderbolts wore aluminum bumpers). Screens took the place of the two inside headlights as those openings were used to feed cooler, denser air directly to the carbs via two huge ducts. A Detroit Locker rearend containing 4.56:1 gears and held in place by welded-on traction bars brought up the rear. This '64 Fairlane street machine was built by its owner to Thunderbolt specs and features a modern pro-street narrowed rearend and aftermarket wheels and tires.

track. For the street, Mercury unleashed its Cyclone on mid-sized Comet buyers. Using the "Hi-Po" 289 as its top optional power source, the Comet Cyclone also featured some nice performance-look items, including buckets and a console, a three-spoke sport steering wheel, a dash-mounted tach, and simulated chrome-wheel hubcaps. At the same time, Ford was making a name for itself among the factory super-stock crowd with its Thunderbolt, an 11sec, 427ci-powered light-weight Fairlane that helped Dearborn win 1964's NHRA Manufacturers Cup. Thunder-bolts did a lot for Ford's image at the track, but they couldn't make up for the fact that Fairlanes were rapidly falling behind in the race on Main Street USA.

In 1966, Fairlanes and Comets received all-new sheet metal, as well as big-block power and a sporty GT package. Standard with the GT and GTA (A for automatic) Fair-lanes and Cyclones was the 335hp 390ci FE-series V-8. Bucket seats, heavy-duty suspen-sion, and various dress-up tricks were also included. Not available with the GT equip-ment, but shoehorned into more than fifty '66 Fairlanes was Ford's legendary 425hp 427ci V-8. Created to make the model legal for super-stock drag racing, the 427 Fairlane appeared again in 1967, joined by equally mighty 427 Comets.

Ford finally made a major impression on the average performance-minded Joe on the street with an affordable mid-sized muscle machine in 1969, rolling out the Fairlane Cobra in fastback and formal-roof form. Mar-

With a standard oval 427 air cleaner in place of the Thunderbolt air box and twin ducts, the 427 High Riser's tall manifold and twin 720cfm Holley four-barrels can be seen. High Riser cylinder heads featured large, "tall" ports, and creating a matching High Riser intake allowed fuel/air mixture a more direct path from the carbs to the combustion chambers. But it also made hood clearance impossible, thus the reason for the trademark teardrop hood. Fitting the 427 into the Fairlane's engine bay required cutting down the shock towers, which were then reinforced with welded steel plates.

keted as a budget-conscious super car along the lines of Plymouth's Road Runner, the Cobra featured few frills, but was powered by a standard 335hp courtesy of the 428 Cobra Jet V-8. In 1970, the Cobra became an upscale Torino model and traded its 428 CJ for the new 429 Thunder Jet. Armed with the optional 375hp 429 Super Cobra Jet, the '70

Cobra ranked as one of Ford's all-time hottest offerings, running the quarter in 13.63sec according to *Super Stock* magazine. Although the optional 429 Cobra Jet was still around in 1971, standard Torino Cobra power came from a 351 Cleveland small-block, an able performer but an imposter in the minds of big-block buyers.

By 1972, Detroit's mid-sized muscle game was all but over, with Ford's Cleveland-powered Gran Torino serving only to preserve powerful memories for a few more years.

Left
Additional weight was trimmed from a Thunderbolt by deleting insulation and sound deadener. Lightweight buckets and a rubber floor mat did away with a few pounds as well. Plexiglass replaced side and rear glass, and the rear quarter window winding mechanisms were deleted. Thunderbolts were equipped with either four-speeds or Lincoln automatic transmissions.

Right
Production of '66 427 Fairlanes—identified externally only by two small fender emblems—totalled but fifty-seven cars. For 1967, Ford extended the 427 option into the top-line XL ranks (GTs were still not available) and a few automatic-equipped 427 Fairlanes were also included among the 163 '67models built. Standard in 1966, the lift-off fiberglass hood with its functional scoop became a 427 Fairlane option in 1967.

With performance being the main intention, all '66 427 Fairlanes were Plain Jane machines throughout, as this bench seat interior attests. All were four-speed cars (automatics weren't available) and all had their heaters and radios deleted.

Right
Buyers interested in equipping a FoMoCo intermediate with 427 power in 1967 were actually presented with a choice or two, a situation contrary to the '66 427 Fairlane which basically presented a take-it-or-leave-it proposition. White was no longer the only color, and Mercury customers were also invited to the party as the 427 made its way into '67 Mercs ranging from the low-priced Comet 202 all the way up to the top-dog Cyclone. According to Ford Motor Company records, only eight '67 Cyclones were produced using R-code and W-code 427s.

Left
Choosing the 410hp 427 added about $900 to a Cyclone sticker in 1967 (the 425hp 427 cost nearly $1,130). Along with the big FE-series V-8, additional race-ready equipment included front disc brakes, an 11.5in heavy-duty clutch, a top-loader four-speed, and a nodular 9in rearend containing beefy thirty-one-spline axles and 3.89:1 gears. Extra cooling was supplied by a larger radiator with a clutch fan, and a 42-amp alternator and heavy-duty battery were also included.

Being an upscale Cyclone, this '67 427 Mercury offers a bit more pizzazz inside in comparison to the more mundane '66 427 Fairlane. Standard Cyclone features included bucket seats and a simulated wood-rimmed steering wheel. This Jamaican Yellow 427 Cyclone even has a radio and a clock.

In standard form, the '69 Fairlane Cobra was indeed an "economy supercar," as the press called it nearly twenty-five years ago. Base price for the rarely seen formal roof variety was $3,206, making it one of the best bangs for the buck in its day (the more popular fastback was even cheaper at $3,183). Armed with a 335hp 428 Cobra Jet V-8 backed by a four-speed, the Fairlane Cobra was an easy mid-14sec stoplight warrior. Adding the optional Ram-Air equipment, which made the Cobra's hood scoop functional, lowered ETs into the low 14sec range. Hood pins and a black-out grille were also included in the deal.

Preceding pages
Introduced in 1966 with standard big-block power, the Fairlane GT took a step backward in 1967 as the 335hp 390ci V-8 was exchanged for the 289 Challenger V-8 small-block. Top power option in '67 was the 320hp 390. GT features included power front disc brakes, a black-out grille, "GT" identification, bucket seats, and a sporty "power dome" hood. The attractive styled steel wheels were optional. Adding the optional Selectshift Cruise-O-Matic C6 automatic transmission transformed a Fairlane GT into a GTA. Total production for '67 GT and GTA hardtops was 18,670; convertibles numbered 2,117.

Fairlane Cobra buyers had but one choice under the hood, but no one was complaining. Heart of this snake was Ford's famed 428 Cobra Jet, conservatively rated at 335hp. Maximum torque was 445lb-ft at 3400rpm with 10.7:1 compression. The large rubber "doughnut" sealed the air cleaner to the hood's underside as part of the optional Ram-Air package. Ram-Air didn't change advertised output, but the improvement was easily recorded by the seat of your pants.

The Fairlane Cobra's staggered rear shocks helped the leaf spring rear suspension stay tight during hard launches. Early Fairlane Cobras apparently carried large Cobra decals, but most models you'll see wear small cast Cobra emblems on each front fender and the deck lid. Options on this Black Jade '69 Cobra include the vinyl roof, chrome styled steel wheels, power front disc brakes, and power steering. For 1970 and '71, Cobras were based on Ford's top-line intermediate, the Torino.

Aerodynamic in 1967 meant all the vertical surfaces were angled as though bent by the wind.

—Randy Leffingwell, *American Muscle*

A four-speed stick was standard Fairlane Cobra equipment in 1969, but practically everything else you see was optional, including the sport steering wheel, bucket seats and console, AM/FM stereo, and 6000rpm tach.

Other than its blacked-out hood and contrasting upper body stripe (not visible in this photo), a '69 Talladega received no other special exterior cosmetic identification save for "T" badges above the door handles and another large "T" on the dummy gas cap in back. NASCAR-inspired tricks also included special rocker panels that were rolled up one inch (at great expense) to create a higher measuring point for inspection officials, meaning track-ready Talladega bodies could be lowered and still stay within legal limits.

Following pages
Built with NASCAR superspeedways in mind, Ford's '69 Talladega may have looked a bit odd with its extended snout, but guffaws quickly faded once this aerodynamic beast hit the track. NASCAR rules required Detroit's automakers to build at least 500 street-going examples of any given bodystyle to make that bodystyle legal for competition. Ford ended up building 745 Talladegas. A flush grille, a modified Fairlane rear bumper, and fender extensions accompanied by a sloping header panel transformed the '69 Talladega's frontend into a wind-cheating airfoil. Mercury tried the same tactic in 1969 with its Cyclone Spoiler II.

Although actual NASCAR racing versions of the Talladega were powered by the Boss 429 powerplant—itself homologated for competition as a Mustang model option—streetside versions were all equipped with 335hp 428 Cobra Jet V-8s backed by C6 automatics. Although brochures mentioned optional Ram-Air, it is believed only two prototypes were built with a functional hood scoop. Talladegas also featured a nodular 9in rear with 3.25:1 gears and thirty-one-spline axles. Included as well were staggered rear shocks, features that came standard on four-speed Cobra Jet Fords

Extending the Talladega's nose required a mini-maze of braces and supports in front of the radiator bulkhead. Hanging out about five inches beyond stock Fairlane specs, the Talladega's front bumper was a Fairlane rear unit cut up and rewelded in a "V" configuration.

Chapter 3

Big Cubes In Big Cars

Fast Full-Sized Fords

While Dearborn was abiding by the 1957 AMA ruling limiting factory performance, GM divisions in the late fifties were busy behind the scenes developing quite an array of hot hardware—the prowess of which was demonstrated by multiple high-profile victories on NASCAR tracks. But just when it seemed Pontiac and Chevrolet would run away and hide, Ford put itself back in the race.

On April 27, 1959, Dearborn officials both informed their GM counterparts of a plan to market high-performance options and suggested everyone take a second look at the AMA agreement. Meanwhile, a three-man team working under the guise of "law enforcement parts development" had set out to put Ford back on the performance track. Included were engineers Dave Evans, Don Sullivan, and John Cowley. The fruit of their labor was Ford's first factory-delivered muscle car powerplant, the 352 Interceptor Special V-8, an FE-series big-block displacing 352ci. Priced at $125, the optional Interceptor Special featured a hot solid-lifter cam, 10.6:1 compression, a dual-point distributor, and an aluminum four-barrel intake. Advertised output was 360hp.

In 1961, the 352 was bored and stroked out to 390ci and maximum horsepower jumped to 375. Later in the year, an optional triple-carb setup was made available over dealer parts counters, as was Ford's first floor-

Opposite page
Ford's last full-sized performance model was the Galaxie XL GT, offered in 1968 and '69. Originally priced at $204.64, the GT equipment group included heavy-duty suspension, power front discs, low-restriction dual exhausts, wide-oval rubber, mag-type wheel covers, GT emblems, and special body side "C-stripes." A 390ci FE-series big-block V-8 was the XL GT's standard power source, but this '69 model is equipped with the optional 429ci 385-series big-block.

Long, low, and wide, Ford's all-new flagship for 1960 was the Starliner coupe, a boulevard cruiser that actually measured 1.5-inches wider than federal highway standards allowed. Equipped with the optional 360hp 352 Interceptor Special V-8, a '60 Starliner basically became Dearborn's first muscle car. At Ford's Romeo, Michigan test track, a 360hp prototype managed 152.6mph, leading *Hot Rod*'s Ray Brock to conclude that though " . . . it took several years, we think Ford has the right answer for 1960."

shifted four-speed transmission. When topped by the three Holley two-barrels, the 390's output was listed at 401hp.

Both the four-on-the-floor and the triple carbs became regular factory options in 1962. Also new for '62 was the 406ci FE big-block, yet another bore-job introduced in December 1961. More ruggedly constructed throughout, the 406 was offered in two forms, a 385hp version with a single four-barrel and the 405hp beast with the triple Holleys. Immediately after the 406 debuted, Ford announced the XL trim package to showcase its hot performance powerplants. Including various exterior dress-up pieces and a sporty bucket seat interior, the Galaxie XL instantly became Ford's flagship. Mercury also made the same mid-year move, rolling out its S-55 Monterey.

The Total Performance campaign kicked into high gear in 1963 as Dearborn designers introduced aerodynamics to their full-sized lineup. Yet another mid-year move attached a sweeping "fastback" to the Galaxie body, making it far more formidable on NASCAR super-speedways. And to help move that big body, engineers beefed up the FE block one more time, resulting in the famed 427. Offered in basically the same form from early 1963 through 1966, the 427 pumped out 425hp with dual four-barrel carbs, or 410hp when fed by a single Holley four-barrel. Appearing briefly for the last time in 1968, a detuned 427 was rated at 390hp.

Kings of NASCAR in 1963 and 1964, the 427 Galaxie's thunder began to fade once intermediate muscle cars hit the scene led by

On December 15, 1961, Ford announced a bigger and better FE-series big-block, the 406. Increasing the 390's bore in a recast, beefed-up block produced the 406, which was offered with one four-barrel carburetor or three Holley two-barrels. Output was 385hp and 405hp, respectively. Compression went as high as 11.4:1. The list of bright dress-up items for the top performance 406s was extensive, including the valve covers, master cylinder cap, fan shroud, radiator cap, dipstick, oil filler cap, and fuel filter.

Pontiac's GTO. Although still available from 1965 through 1967, full-sized 427s were rarely seen. In a move to renew interest in powerful big cars, Ford introduced its 7-Litre Galaxie in 1966, a model offering more pizzazz than actual performance. Standard 7-Litre power came from a 345hp 428ci big-block V-8, the final displacement variation on the FE-series theme. After relatively disappointing sales, the 7-Litre was demoted from full model line status to optional sport package in 1967. Few buyers noticed.

Ford's last shot at full-sized performance came in 1968 when Dearborn's better idea guys finally stuck GT badges on Galaxie fenders. Available only for big-block XLs, the optional GT equipment group helped distract buyers from the fact that sporty XL models no longer came with bucket seats and V-8 power as standard equipment. In 1969, the XL's sleek, new SportsRoof fastback body sweetened the GT pot considerably, as did the optional 360hp 429ci 385-series big-block V-8. Although the 429 would carry on, the '69 XL GT effectively ended Ford's big car performance bloodline.

Introduced in June 1962, the sporty XL package was created to help showcase Ford's hottest full-sized performance powerplants. Along with various exterior trim pieces, the top-line XLs featured front buckets, console and floor shifter, and an engine-turned dash insert. The '62 XL's factory-installed four-speed with floor shifter was a first for Ford; in 1961 an optional four-on-the-floor had debuted mid-year, but it was only available as a dealer-installed item.

Sitting two inches lower than its '62 forerunner, the '63-1/2 "fastback" Galaxie was a reported 28 percent more aerodynamic—a fact that instantly translated into major success on NASCAR's superspeedways. Recognizing that the "notchback" Galaxie profile was a veritable brick at high speeds, Ford's idea guys had tried to get away with attaching an optional "Starlift" roof to the '62 convertible to create a more swoopy shape for NASCAR competition. NASCAR rules moguls, however, didn't buy the idea, forcing Ford designers back to the drawing board. The result was this stylish, functional, mid-year bodystyle. To power the new fastback Galaxie, Ford engineers again beefed up the FE block, this time boring it out to 427ci—at least that's what they said. Actual displacement computed to 425ci, but Dearborn's image-makers apparently didn't want Ford's top performance powerplant to take a back seat to rival offerings. Seven liters, or roughly 427ci, was the established legal limit for stock-class racing, and with a flick of a public relations pen the new 425ci big-block was introduced to the public as being right at that limit. Triple carbs were dropped for 1963 in favor of two big Holley four-barrels. Counting both the single-carb 410hp and the dual-carb 425hp versions, Ford sold 4,978 427-equipped models in 1963.

Preceding pages

Undoubtedly the most prominent of the full-sized 427s was the '64 Galaxie. This was due largely to its overwhelming success on the 1964 NASCAR circuit where Ford garnered thirty wins, fifteen of those by Galaxie pilot Ned Jarrett. As in 1962 and 1963, Dearborn also built a special run of light-weight '64 Galaxies for A/Stock and B/Stock drag racing. Beneath a fiberglass, teardrop-scooped hood, A/Stock Galaxies were powered by a 427 High Riser, while the B/Stock cars used the "tamer" 427 Low Riser.

Identified only by two small front fender emblems, 427 Galaxies left many a streetside challenger wondering what hit him in 1964. All 427 Galaxies built in '63 and '64 were four-speed cars. Automatics were not available, though some '64 lightweight drag cars—like the Fairlane Thunderbolts—were fitted with Lincoln automatics. Equipped with 3.25:1 highway gears, a typical street-stock '64 427 Galaxie ran 0–60mph in 7.1sec and turned a 13.96sec quarter-mile during a *Speed & Custom* test.

Beneath that trademark oval air cleaner hide two 652cfm Holley four-barrel carburetors on an aluminum intake. Rated at 425hp, the dual-carb "R-code" 427 featured streamlined cast-iron headers, 11.5:1 compression, cross-bolted four-bolt main bearing caps, a solid-lifter cam, and chrome valve covers. Torque output was 480lb-ft at 3700rpm.

W hat it is is lightning without thunder. It *moves*—but it moves like mist over a millpond, smoothly, quietly, effortlessly!

—Ford 7-Litre advertisement, 1965

Performance-look accessories were of little concern to 427 Ford buyers in 1964, and additional gadgetry such as a tach and gauges weren't available. Not being a top-line XL model, this 427 Galaxie 500 features a somewhat spartan bench seat interior.

Ads called the '66 7-Litre "either the quickest quiet car or the quietest quick car." Demonstrating that full-sized performance was already a thing of the past, the 1966 7-Litre was basically a sporty boulevard cruiser offering more luxury than performance. Standard equipment included front disc brakes and a 345hp 428ci engine. According to *Car Life*, a 345hp/C6 automatic 7-Litre could do no better than a 16.9sec ET in the quarter, a far cry from the 14sec runs clocked by '65 427 Galaxies. The optional 425hp 427 promised more bang for the buck, but reportedly only thirty-eight '66 7-Litres, including one convertible, were equipped with the king of the FEs.

Though it didn't make much difference, as the competition was doing it as well, the big Fords got bigger, gaining pounds and inches on a yearly basis.

—Phil Hall, *Fearsome Fords*

Along with this grille badge, standard 7-Litre exterior identification included similar emblems on the fenders and deck lid, body side striping, and mag-style wheel covers. The 7-Litre's die-cast aluminum grille is a standard Galaxie XL feature. Ford built 2,368 7-Litre convertibles for 1966; hardtop production was 8,705.

Left
Bucket seats, Ford's new Cruise-O-Matic C6 automatic transmission, a console with floor shifter, and a simulated wood-rimmed sport steering wheel were standard 7-Litre features. Optional equipment shown here includes a reclining passenger seat and the "Safety Convenience Control Panel," which houses five warning lights as a unit just above the console. Ford's top-loader four-speed manual was also available at extra cost, but apparently only 20 percent of 7-Litre buyers chose to do their own shifting.

A model series all its own in 1966, the 7-Litre was transformed into a mere options group in '67. Priced at $515.86, the "7-Litre Sport Package" again included the 345hp 428 backed by a C6 automatic, power front discs, and the bucket seat XL interior with a sport steering wheel. Although factory photos showed a twin-scooped hood and small, round fender emblems, most 7-Litres apparently carried no specific exterior identification save for the "428" fender badges. The familiar mag-style wheel covers were standard features in '66, but optional in '67. Approximately fifty 7-Litres were built in '67.

Opposite page
Essentially mechanically identical to the '66 7-Litre's standard 345hp 428, the '67 7-Litre powerplant featured chrome valve covers, which had been painted blue in 1966 like the open-element air cleaner. As in '66, the truly powerful 427 was a 7-Litre option in 1967.

This particular '67 7-Litre hardtop carries only one special piece of identification—this steering wheel hub medallion. Since any '67 Galaxie could have been ordered with a 428 V-8, the front fender badges did not necessarily denote the presence of a 7-Litre.

Left
Along with hideaway headlights, top-line XL models for 1969 received an exciting new "SportsRoof" shape featuring a recessed rear window. Combining the fresh XL face with the sporty GT equipment resulted in what Dearborn's advertising crew called "the Michigan strong boy." Ford's "sleek, solid, and silent" XL GT was also offered in convertible form. Popular options included a choice between a four-speed manual or SelectShift Cruise-O-Matic automatic, a limited-slip rearend, buckets seats, and a console.

In base form, a '69 XL GT was powered by a 265hp 390ci big-block V-8 topped by a two-barrel carburetor. Available at extra cost were two 429 big-blocks, one with a two-barrel (2V), the other with a four-barrel (4V). Output for the 429-2V was 320hp; the 429-4V made 360hp. In reference to the latter, Ford brochures claimed, "With 480 pounds of torque, this optional muscle machine could move a mountain"—a fair description considering the '69 XL GT weighed 4,135 pounds.

Chapter 4

Powered by Ford

Other Dearborn Developments

Although the 360hp 1960 Starliner may be considered Ford's first muscle car, Dearborn's performance tale actually began a few years earlier. A hot parts program had just gotten off the ground in 1957 when the infamous Automobile Manufacturers Association "ban" on factory racing shot it down. Early in the year, both Ford's regular passenger cars and its glamourous two-seat Thunderbirds had appeared with top performance versions of the 312ci Y-block V-8. Potent options included a dual-carb intake, radical cam kits, and a Paxton-built supercharger. But all that heavy-duty hardware quickly became museum pieces in February 1957 when the AMA moved to pull in the reins on Detroit's rapidly escalating horsepower race.

Another hot Thunderbird wouldn't appear until 1962, after Ford re-introduced the two-seat theme. With a special tonneau cover hiding its back seats, the Sports Roadster T-bird looked every bit the part of a performance machine. And with the optional "M-code" triple-carb 390ci V-8 beneath the hood, a Sports Roadster did feel mightier than the average 'Bird. Built in both 1962 and 1963, the M-code Thunderbird represented the last combination of personal luxury and performance.

Opposite page
A pair of Carroll Shelby's aces—the 289 Cobra (left) and its awesome 427ci variant. Featuring various competition modifications, this white small-block Cobra also wears FIA racing sheet metal—standard street versions of the 260 and 289 Cobras did not include the flaring needed to clear the wide racing rubber. Modifications required to fit the 427 in place of the 289 included a heavily reinforced chassis and coil springs at all four corners instead of the front and rear transverse leaf springs. The aluminum body's width grew seven inches thanks to the huge flares, and a more aggressive-looking snout with a larger grille opening was added to improve cooling.

To most minds, the '57 two-seat Thunderbird was a wonderfully classy personal luxury automobile, a vehicle perfect for a night on the town or a demonstration of status at the club. But a sports car it wasn't, although Ford initially offered two performance options to help put the thunder in Thunderbird. Known today by its serial number identification, the E-code '57 T-bird featured a 270hp 312ci Y-block V-8 with two four-barrel carburetors, while the F-code version replaced the two Holleys with a single Holley four-barrel force fed through a McCulloch centrifugal supercharger supplied by Paxton. Output for the blown 'Bird was 300hp, or 340hp with the optional NASCAR "racing kit."

While the Thunderbird was leaving performance behind, a former race driver from Texas was helping pick up the slack. Determined to build his own sports car after competing in others' for nearly ten years, Carroll Shelby had abandoned his racing career in 1960—thanks in part to a heart condition—and began seeking a new career as an automaker. In 1962, he combined a British sports car, the AC Ace, with Ford's new thin-wall-cast V-8, resulting in Shelby American's first AC Cobra, described by *Sports Car Graphic*'s editors as "one of the most impressive production sports cars we've ever driven." They spoke too soon. In 1963, Shelby replaced the 260ci V-8 with the enlarged 289ci version, then proceeded to squeeze every ounce of performance out of Dearborn's Windsor small-block. Race-ready 289 Cobras reportedly reached nearly 400hp, but even that wasn't enough.

In late 1964, Shelby unleashed his outrageous 427 Cobra. With huge Girling disc brakes at all four corners and 425 horses of FE-series big-block power beneath its aluminum skin, the 427 Cobra could rocket from rest to 100mph and back in 14.5sec. "That figure," reported *Car and Driver*, "is obtainable by the average Cobra driver with the regular 8.15x15 Goodyear Blue Dot street tires. [Shelby American racer] Ken Miles has done the job in as little as 13.8 seconds, and who knows how much improvement could be made with racing tires that would nullify some of the tremendous wheel spin?" There could be only one king of the American road in the sixties, and the 427 Cobra was it.

Along with helping create the 427 Cobra, Ken Miles had also assisted another British sport car builder with its Anglo-American hybrid. In April 1963, Miles had teamed with Britain's Rootes Motors to build a V-8-equipped Sunbeam Alpine prototype using Ford's 260ci small-block. Once refined, the Sunbeam Tiger emerged as what some considered the "poor man's Cobra." Later in December 1966, the 260 was replaced by a 200hp 289, with only 633 of the more powerful Mk II Tigers rolling off the Rootes line before production ceased in June 1967.

It was almost dangerous to put the Cobra in a showroom alongside your usual Detroit lead sled in 1964. The salesmen had to be properly educated just to demonstrate the car without killing themselves.

—Wallace A. Wyss,
Shelby's Wildlife

Two years before the Tiger's demise, Shelby American had introduced another Ford-powered street racer, this time using the Mustang as a base. Featuring a 306hp 289ci small-block, the GT350 was better suited to the track than the street, but subsequent renditions were gradually "civilized"—much to Shelby's dismay. In 1967, a second Shelby Mustang—the GT500 with its 428 big-block V-8—debuted to complement the 289-equipped GT350. The following year, Shelby Mustang production moved from Shelby American's Los Angeles facility to the A. O. Smith Company in Livonia, Michigan, with the last GT350s and 500s being built there in 1970.

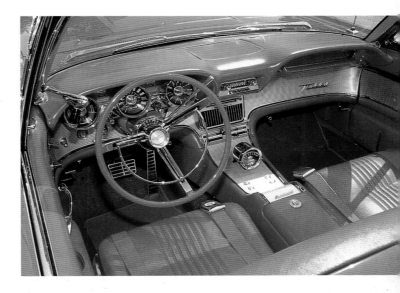

Aftermarket experiments with rear seat tonneau covers began appearing almost immediately after Ford had introduced the larger four-place Thunderbird in 1958. One of the more successful two-seat conversion efforts came from New Jersey Ford dealer Bill Booth, who also owned a fiberglass fabrication shop. Perhaps inspired by Booth's design, Ford stylist Bud Kaufman created a comparable cover that fit over the '62 Thunderbird's back seats and still allowed the convertible top to operate unheeded. Dearborn offered the Sports Roadster package as a factory option for '62; in '64 the attractive cover remained available as a dealer-installed feature.

Left
In 1962, Ford responded to requests for a return to the two-seat T-bird image by rolling out the Sports Roadster, a lavish showboat priced at a hefty $5,439. Included in the deal was a fiberglass tonneau cover with twin headrests that transformed the four-place 'Bird into a dream machine built for two. A dash-mounted grab bar for the passenger and four dazzling Kelsey-Hayes wire wheels completed the package. Sports Roadster production reached 1,427 in 1962; this '63 model is one of only 455 built. Bottom line for a '63 Sports Roadster was $5,563.

The grab bar on the passenger's side of the dash was included as part of the Sports Roadster package. Power steering and brakes, the three-speed Cruise-O-Matic automatic transmission, and the Swing-Away steering wheel were all standard Thunderbird features in 1963. With the transmission in park and the door open, the wheel would swing 10.5-inches to the left, allowing easy access. The wheel locked back in place once the transmission was shifted into drive.

To enhance the Sports Roadster's performance image, Ford engineers added a unique triple-carb intake to the Thunderbird's 390ci FE big-block V-8. Topped by three Holley two-barrels, the "M-code" aluminum manifold differed from the passenger car tri-carb setup due to the

Thunderbird's "flat" engine position. A Galaxie V-8 slanted backward, meaning its intake was stair-stepped to keep the carburetors level; an M-code 390 manifold mounted all three carbs at the same height. Available for all Thunderbirds, the M-code 390 was rated at 340hp. Total

After seeing Carroll Shelby's success with his AC Cobra, officials from Great Britain's Rootes Group began plotting a similar Anglo-American hybrid in the spring of 1963. The resulting Sunbeam Tiger was priced around $3,500, weighed 2500lb, and initially featured a 164hp 260ci Ford small-block V-8. Reportedly, the car could go from rest to 100mph and back in less than 20sec. Regular production of Mk I Tigers began in June 1964. A slightly modified Mk IA was unveiled in August 1965, and the more powerful 289-powered Mk II rolled off the line in December 1966. Total production was 7,083. This '65 260 Tiger is one of 2,694 Mk IA models built.

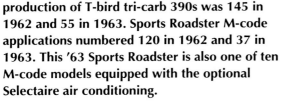

production of T-bird tri-carb 390s was 145 in 1962 and 55 in 1963. Sports Roadster M-code applications numbered 120 in 1962 and 37 in 1963. This '63 Sports Roadster is also one of ten M-code models equipped with the optional Selectaire air conditioning.

With about seventy-five of his 260-powered AC Cobras built, Carroll Shelby made the switch to Ford's larger 289 Windsor small-block in 1963. Right out of the crate, the High Performance 289 was rated at 271hp. A few tweaks and some added compression bumped output even further and helped make the small-block Cobra a sizzling success. According to *Car Life*, a standard 289 Cobra with 3.77:1 gears managed 0–60mph in 5.7sec. Various potent options, such as these four Weber two-barrel carburetors, promised even quicker results.

Right
After Ken Miles had toyed with the idea of stuffing Ford's big 427 into the little Cobra, Shelby American began building big-block competition models in October 1964. Shelby's first completed 427 Cobra, CSX 3002, emerged in January 1965, beating CSX 3001 off the line while it waited for its completely restyled aluminum 427ci body shell. Additional 427 Cobra chassis modifications included widening the rear track 4.5-inches and front track 3.5-inches. From 1965 to 1967, Shelby American unleashed 348 427 Cobras in all-out racing, S/C (semi-competition), and street car forms.

Transforming a 2500lb British sports car into world-class road rocket was as simple as dropping 425hp worth of dual-carb 427ci Ford side-oiler V-8 beneath the bonnet. With 480lb-ft of torque, the 427 big-block transformed the already uncivilized Cobra into a downright savage. During a 1965 *Car and Driver* test, a 427 Cobra smoked the quarter-mile in 12.2sec at 118mph, easily the fastest time ever recorded by an American "production" vehicle.

Right
When first introduced in 1965, Shelby American's GT350 Mustang variant was a single-purpose machine available in one color only, without a back seat or an automatic transmission, and loaded with a full collection of standard race-ready hardware. In 1966, the car was tamed a bit as most of the hottest performance pieces became options and a back seat was added, along with various color choices and an optional C4 automatic. Big news for 1967 was an attractive make-over featuring various fiberglass components, an extended snout, and Cougar sequential taillights. This '67 GT350 lacks the popular dealer-installed Le Mans stripes, which ran parallel down the hood, roof, and deck lid.

Left
Shelby GT350 interior features included a Hurst shifter, a wood-rimmed sport steering wheel, an underdash gauge pod, an 8000rpm tachometer, and a 140mph speedometer. Shelby American built 1,175 small-block GT350s in 1967.

Heart of the GT350 from 1965 until 1967 was the Shelby-modified High Performance 289. Although the tri-Y headers used in '65 and '66 were exchanged for standard Ford cast-iron exhaust manifolds, advertised output for the "Cobra-ized" 289 remained at 306hp. Helping boost output from Ford's standard rating of 271hp was a 715cfm Holley four-barrel on an aluminum high-rise intake.

New for 1967 was a second Shelby Mustang model, the GT500, featuring a 428ci FE-series big-block V-8 as standard equipment. Featuring two 600cfm Holley four-barrels on an aluminum intake, the Shelby 428 was rated at 355hp. Both the GT500 and GT350 received the same styling upgrades, including a fiberglass nose that added three inches to total length. The fiberglass hood with its functional scoop, the lower valance panel, and the grille were all unique '67 Shelby features, as were the twin 7in driving lights. Since some states specified a minimum distance between headlights, many Shelby Mustangs have these lights mounted apart at each end of the grille.

New '67 Shelby bodywork in back included brake-cooling scoops, rear-quarter ventilators, and a duck-tail deck lid with matching rear-quarter spoiler ends, all made of fiberglass. Notice the optional Le Mans stripes. The 15in Mag Star aluminum center/steel rim wheels were also optional. This '67 GT500 is one of 2,050 built. Thanks to the big-block GT500's introduction, Shelby Mustang sales jumped 35 percent for 1967.

Right
Although not officially offered as a Shelby American option in '67, Ford's 425hp 427ci side-oiler V-8 did find its way into a few '67 GT500s. With only half of Shelby American's factory invoices for 1967 presently available, another two 427 GT500s have been documented. But since any dealer could have made the swap on request and an owner could have requested the change at additional cost if he blew his 428 under warranty, there's no telling how many 427 '67 Shelbys hit the streets. Non-stock items on this 427 include a Mallory distributor and aftermarket headers.

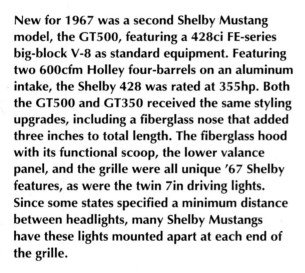

CHEVY
MUSCLE CARS

Acknowledgments

The author would like to thank every car owner whose pride and joy appears within these pages. It was the cooperation, patience, and, above all, hospitality of each of them that made this book possible. In order of appearance, these lucky men and women are:

Randall and Patti Fort of New Smyrna Beach, FL, (1970 Chevelle SS 454); Roger and David Judski of Roger's Corvette Center, Maitland, FL, (1969 ZL1 and 1967 L88 Corvettes); Ervin Ray of Tavares, FL, (1966 Corvair Turbo Corsa); James Hill of West Palm Beach, FL, (1963 Nova SS convertible); Tom and Nancy Stump of North Liberty, IN, (1967 Nova SS); Dan Bennett and Jim Beckerle of Festus, MO, (1969 Nova SS 396); Steven Conti of St. Petersburg, FL, (1967 SS Camaro convertible); Paul McGuire of Melbourne, FL, (1967 Z/28 Camaro); Jim and Gina Collins of Hollywood, FL, (1967 SS 396 Camaro); Bill and Barbara Jacobsen of Silver Dollar Classic Cars, Odessa, FL, (1968 SS 396 Camaro); Mick Price of Atwood, IL, (1969 Yenko Camaro); Jim Price of La Place, IL, (1969 ZL1 Camaro); Scott Gaulter of Waukee, IA, (1964 Chevelle SS); Floyd Garrett of Fernandina Beach, FL, (1965 Z16 Chevelle SS 396); Bob and Christa Gatchel of Clermont, FL, (1966 SS 396 Chevelle); Roger Adkins of Dresden, TN, (1969 L89 SS 396 300 Deluxe sedan); Fred Knoop of Atherton, CA, (1969 COPO 427 Chevelle)—photo shoot courtesy of Roger Gibson, Roger Gibson Auto Restoration, Kelso, MO; Mick Price of Atwood, IL, (1969 Yenko Chevelle); Lukason and Sons Collection of FL, (1970 LS6 Chevelle convertible); Carl Beck of Clearwater, FL, (1970 SS 396 El Camino); Walter Cutlip of Longwood, FL, (1958 Impala convertible); Marty Locke of Lucasville, OH, (1961 Impala SS 409); Jerry Peeler of Clermont, FL, (1962 Bel Air 409); Frank Ristagno of Philadelphia, PA, (1964 Impala SS 409 convertible); Don Springer of Tampa, FL, (1967 Impala SS 427 convertible); Jim and Carol Collins of Hollywood, FL, (1969 Impala SS 427 convertible); courtesy Sullivan Chevrolet of Champaign, IL, (1970 454 Caprice); John Young of Mulberry, FL, (1954 Corvette); Ed and Diann Kuziel of Tampa, FL, (1962 Corvette); Lukason and Sons Collection of Florida (1965 396 Corvette).

Introduction
The Bow Tie Legacy

Chevrolet's fortunes took a major upswing when the "Hot One" came along in 1955. Featuring the division's first overhead-valve V-8, the famed 1955 Chevy left Chevrolet's tired "Stovebolt" image in the dust as an unbeatable performance reputation was born almost overnight.

Chevrolet's fiberglass two-seater also received Ed Cole's OHV 265 cubic inch V-8 that same year, saving Zora Arkus-Duntov's Corvette from possible extinction. Meanwhile, thanks to Daytona Beach race car builder Smokey Yunick, 1955 Chevys had become formidable forces in NASCAR's short track division. At Yunick's urging, Chevrolet hired long-time performance product manager Vince Piggins in 1956, laying a base for a racing parts program that would help keep Chevy street performance offerings at or near the top of the heap for nearly two decades.

Chevy's small-block V-8 quickly became the hot rodder's choice, as well as a base for countless high-performance factory models. Then along came the 348 cubic inch big-block in 1958, the forerunner of the legendary 409. Introduced in 1961, the 409 roared to many victories on NHRA drag strips under Bel Air and Impala hoods.

By 1965, the full-sized 409s were displaced by lighter, high-powered intermediates. Chevrolet had introduced its A-body model, the Chevelle, for 1964, followed by the 396 cubic inch Mk IV big-block V-8 in 1965. The Mk IV transformed the Corvette into a real screamer, made the Super Sport Chevelle a crowd-pleasing success, and later did the same for the 1967 Camaro and 1968 Nova.

In 1966, the 427 cubic inch Mk IV big-block was born as an option for full-sized models and Corvettes. With Piggins' help, 427s also found their way through the Central Office Production Order (COPO) pipeline into Camaros and Chevelles three years later, despite GM's 400 cubic inch limit for intermediates and

Borrowing the lightweight, stamped steel, ball-stud rocker arm design created by Pontiac engineers, Chevrolet's 265 cubic inch overhead-valve V-8 was a high-winding powerplant with loads of potential. Introduced in 1955, the first in a long line of Chevy small-block V-8s, it was rated at 180 horsepower with a four-barrel carb and dual exhausts.

pony cars. (GM had passed an anti-racing edict in 1963 and was trying to downplay performance.) The ZL1 aluminum 427 Camaro and L72 cast-iron 427 Chevelle, both limited edition COPO creations built for 1969, stand among Chevrolet's hottest products, surpassed only by the 1967–1969 L88 aluminum head 427 Corvettes and their more exotic 1969 ZL1 427 siblings—all impressive, but well beyond the average customer's reach.

On a more realistic scale, 1970 was the pinnacle year for Chevrolet performance. This was due in no small part to the lifting of the 400 cubic inch limit for its smaller model lines and the resulting creation of the SS 454 Chevelle. In 450 horsepower LS6 trim, the 1970 SS 454 may well have represented Detroit's strongest regular-production muscle car, with low 13-second quarter-mile runs possible right off the truck.

But by 1971, tightening federal emissions standards had brought on drastically lowered

Two of Chevrolet's most powerful offerings, the 1967 L88 (in back) and 1969 ZL1 Corvettes. Both cars were drastically underrated at 430 horsepower, with more than 500 horses at the ready from both the aluminum head L88 and all-aluminum ZL1 427 big-block V-8s. While a mere twenty L88 Corvettes were built for 1967, only two ZL1s were produced two years later.

compression ratios and stifling pollution control equipment. Detroit's muscle car era came to an end in a morass of rising insurance rates and escalating safety and environmental concerns. Chevrolet's street performance legacy basically went dormant after 1972, re-emerging less than a decade later when technology began to meet the demands of the modern performance market.

Perhaps Detroit's most popular muscle car, Chevrolet's Super Sport Chevelle reached the pinnacle in SS 454 form for 1970. In base trim, the SS 454 featured the 360 horsepower LS5 454 cubic inch big-block. The king of the hill, however, was the LS6, which pumped out 450 horsepower worth of mid-sized muscle.

Chapter 1

Big Guns
Full-Sized Flyers from 409 to 454

In the beginning—before Camaros, before Chevelles, before Sting Rays—there was the 409, Chevrolet's legendary, lyrical, performance powerplant. When the 409 was introduced in 1961, big cubes in big cars represented the only way to fly as Detroit's muscle car wars were just beginning to heat up. For Chevy, escalation had begun in 1958, the year engineers transformed the 348 "W-head" truck engine into the first beefed-up Bow Tie big-block V-8. With triple two-barrel carbs, the 348 initially maxed out at 315 horsepower, but by 1961 it was producing 350 horses.

That same year, Chevy engineers upped the ante again, recasting the W-head V-8's block to make room for 409 cubic inches. And to showcase the new 360 horsepower 409, Chevrolet introduced the Impala Super Sport, a classy hardtop that would reign supreme as one of the 1960s top full-sized performers.

In typical fashion, the 409 progressed up the performance ladder each year, receiving two four-barrel carbs in 1962 to raise output to 409 horsepower, then reaching a maximum of 425 horsepower in 1963. But by 1965, the coming of the 396 cubic inch Mk IV big-block V-8 spelled the end for the antiquated 409, which had dropped to 400 horses in top tune. Production of 400- and 340-horsepower 409s for 1965 reached 2,828, bringing the five-year total to 43,755.

Introduced midyear in 1965, the 396 cubic inch big-block helped diehards forget all about the 409. Offered in two forms, 325- and 425-horsepower, the 396 Mk IV was an instant suc-

Once Chevrolets began putting on considerable weight in the late 1950s, engineers responded with more horsepower and torque. Beginning in 1958, the additional power came courtesy of the 348 cubic inch "W-head" V-8. Also introduced in 1958, Chevy's decked-out Impala weighed as much as 300lb more than the previous year's topliner, the 1957 Bel Air.

cess, reaching sales of nearly 60,000 for the year. In 1966, another Mk IV big-block was introduced as the 396 was bored and stroked to 427 cubic inches, identical to the Mk IV's forefather, the Mk II "Mystery Motor" that had first appeared for NASCAR action at Daytona in February 1963. Although maximum 427 output, at 425 horses, was the same as the 396, that power was achieved at 800 less rpm.

Chevrolet's top Mk IV big-block was an option for all full-sized 1966 models and became the star of the Impala Super Sport line in 1967 with the arrival of the SS 427. Offered along with the standard Impala SS, the SS 427 reappeared in 1968, and again in 1969, as the last of the full-sized Super Sports. Although the SS imagery was gone, buyers of full-sized Chevys in 1970 could still order the 390 horsepower 454, and in 1971 the detuned 365 horsepower 454 remained available. By then, however, luxury was the main selling point as big car performance had long since faded away.

The 348 was originally designed for truck duty and is easily recognized by its valve covers, which resemble a *W* or an *M* depending on your perspective. With one four-barrel carburetor and 9.5:1 compression, Chevy's first Turbo-Thrust 348 was rated at 250 horsepower. Exchanging the four-barrel for three Rochester two-barrels upped output to 280 horsepower. At the top was the maximum performance Super Turbo-Thrust 348 featuring a solid-lifter Duntov cam, 11:1 compression, and the same three Rochesters; output was 315 horses.

Introduced shortly after the famed 409 made the performance scene early in 1961, the Impala Super Sport represented icing on the cake. Chevrolet's Super Sport kit, an optional package for the Impala line (originally, brochures even advertised a stillborn four-door model), was rolled out to showcase the new 409, though the venerable 348 was an available 1961 SS power source. Exterior SS treatment included spinner wheel covers and "SS" badges on the rear quarters and deck lid. Only 453 1961 Impala Super Sports were built; 409 production for 1961 was a mere 142 units.

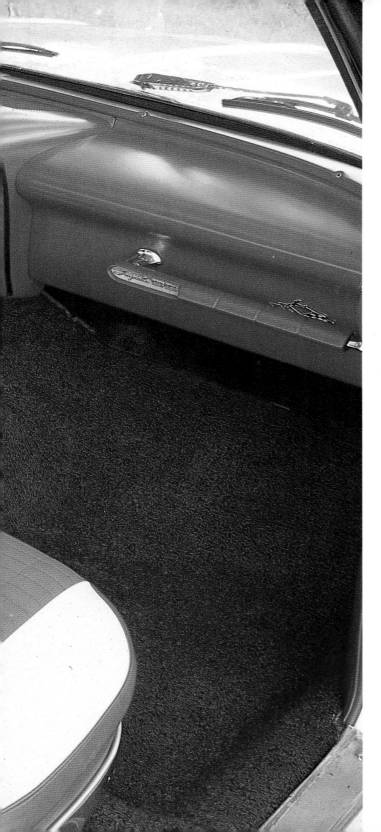

Although nearly identical in outward appearance to its 348 forerunner, the 1961 409 was quite different internally with a beefier block, forged aluminum pistons, and a more aggressive solid-lifter cam. Compression was 11.25:1; output was 360 horsepower at 5800rpm. Fuel/air was supplied by a Carter four-barrel on an aluminum intake that was painted in early cars despite the fact that the paint quickly peeled. Dressed up with chrome by many owners, the 1961 409 was originally delivered with painted valve covers and air cleaners. This 409 is incorrectly equipped with a 348 single-snorkel air cleaner; 1961 409s had dual-snorkel units.

Left
Super Sport interior modifications included a sport steering wheel with a column-mounted 7000rpm tachometer, a Corvette-style grab bar on the passenger side of the dash, and a bright floor plate housing the shifter in four-speed cars.

113

Although the preferred 409 application for the sake of image was the Super Sport Impala, drag racers were better off choosing the lighter, less expensive Bel Air "bubbletop" coupe. Nineteen sixty-two Bel Airs—like this 409 horsepower dual-quad 409 version—were a common sight in NHRA winners' circles.

In 1962, revised heads and a hotter cam upped 409 output to 380 horsepower with a single four-barrel carburetor. Priced at $428, the 380 horsepower 409 was only the beginning. Sixty dollars more added twin Carter AFBs, increasing the 409's advertised maximum rating to 409 horsepower at 6000rpm. Painted valve covers were the norm in 1962; in 1963 chrome dress-up became standard 409 fare. Total production of 1962 409s was 15,019.

She's real fine, my 409.
　　　　　—The Beach Boys, *409*

The most outrageous 409 was the Z11 factory drag package, which first appeared in very limited numbers in late 1962 for NHRA A/FX competition. Z11 components included replacement heads, pistons, and cam for the 409 horsepower 409, along with a special two-piece intake manifold. Also included were aluminum fenders, inner fenders, and hood. In 1963, aluminum front and rear bumpers were added to the Z11 option group, as was a special 409 stroked to 427 cubic inches. The 1963 Z11 was easily identified by its NASCAR-style cowl plenum air cleaner setup. Laughably underrated at 430 horsepower, the Z11's actual output was more than 500 horses.

Right
The distinctive anodized aluminum bodyside trim pieces with their swirl pattern had become a Super Sport trademark in 1962, but truly stood out running down the bodyside of a 1964 Impala SS. Easily the most popular among Detroit's sporty full-sized crowd, the 1964 Super Sport attracted 185,325 buyers. This 409-equipped 1964 SS convertible features the optional wire wheel covers in place of the familiar flat Super Sport spinners.

In 1963 and 1964, Chevrolet offered three different 409s. At the top was the dual-quad 425 horsepower version, RPO L80. Next down the ladder was the single-carb 400 horsepower L31. Tamest of the bunch, and the only 409 available with an automatic transmission, was the 340 horsepower L33. This 1964 L33 V-8 was one of 8,864 409s built for 1964, down from a high of 16,902 the previous year.

Right
New for 1967 was a Super Sport package built specifically around an engine option: the Impala SS 427. Powered by the 385 horsepower 427, the 1967 SS 427 was offered in hardtop or convertible form and featured heavy-duty suspension, a special domed hood, a blacked-out rear cove panel with "SS 427" identification, and unique "SS 427" crossflags on the front fenders. Only 2,124 of these high-priced, high-powered showboats were built.

Included with the SS 427 package, and optional on other 1967 Chevys, the L36 427 produced a maximum 385 horses at 5200rpm; maximum torque was 460lb-ft at 3400rpm. Compression was 10.25:1. Even with all that torque, throwing a two-ton 1967 Impala around was no easy task. According to *Car Life*, a 1967 SS 427 went 0–60mph in 8.4 seconds; quarter-mile time was 15.75 seconds at 86.5mph.

Right
The last Impala Super Sport came in 1969, and it went out with a bang as the SS 427 was the only model offered. Absent was a special domed hood (used in 1967) and fender "gills" (a 1968 SS 427 feature); in their place were large "SS" fender badges and a custom grille. Nearly unnoticeable "427" badges were incorporated with the front fender marker lights. Production for the last of the three SS 427 models was 2,455.

Listed under RPO Z24, the SS 427 package for 1969 included this 390 horsepower 427 Turbo-Jet. Mildly modified cylinder heads and pistons made for a five horsepower increase compared to the 1967 and 1968 L36s. Maximum torque remained the same at 460lb-ft, but came 2000rpm higher at 3600 revs.

As standard equipment under an SS 454 Chevelle's bulging hood, the LS5 454 was rated at 365 horsepower. In full-sized applications, Chevy's LS5 carried the Corvette's 390 horsepower output rating. At 500lb-ft, torque output was the same for all LS5 applications, as were 10.25:1 pistons.

S S 427: just the ticket for the sporting man who likes some room to move around in.

—1967 Chevrolet advertisement

By 1970, the Super Sports were gone but an Impala or Caprice customer in search of full-sized performance could still check off Chevy's biggest big-blocks as an option. This Caprice sport coupe is powered by the LS5 454. Along with all that big-block brute force, this Caprice also features many of the comforts of home, from power door locks, seats, and windows, to a tilt wheel and AM/FM stereo. Performance options include the 15in Rally wheels, F40 sport suspension, and G80 positraction rear end.

Chapter 2

Mighty Mites
Corvairs and Novas

Chevrolet performance models came in all shapes and sizes, not the least of which were the compact Corvairs and Chevy IIs. Introduced in 1960 and 1962, respectively, both models were initially offered as budget-minded competition aimed at the foreign compacts that had gained a foothold in the American market in the late 1950s.

Many customers, however, looked at the Corvair as a Euro-style sportster. In 1961, 42.5 percent chose the optional bucket seats, followed by 64.6 percent in 1962 and 80.5 percent in 1963. By 1965, the only body style available was a sporty hardtop roofline offered in both four- and two-door form. Enhancing the sporty image were various optional performance packages, beginning in 1962 with heavy-duty, sintered-iron brakes, a positraction transaxle, and special handling equipment.

Big news for 1962 was the Monza Spyder, a true performance Corvair powered by a turbocharged version of Chevrolet's air-cooled, 145 cubic inch six-cylinder opposed engine. With 10lb of boost, the turbo upped the pancake six's output to an impressive 150 horsepower. Both convertible and coupe Spyders were produced for three years, though the turbo option carried on after the Spyder's demise. For 1965 and 1966, the turbocharged Corvair Corsa six-cylinder displaced 164 cubic inches and was rated at a healthy 180 horsepower.

The performance angle was initially a bit tougher to come by for Chevy II buyers. No ifs, ands, or buts about it, the first Chevy II was a 100 percent budget buggy with power coming

Along with being the last year for the Chevy II designation, 1968 was also the first year for the SS 396 Nova, which was offered through 1970. Almost identical to its 1968 forerunner, this 1969 SS 396 Nova features optional Rally wheels. SS 396 exterior trim included the blacked-out grille with "SS" badge and "396" identification in the front marker lights.

Although the Monza Spyder had been discontinued after 1964, a turbocharged Corvair was still available in 1965 and 1966. Available only on Corsa hardtops like this 1966, the turbocharger option featured no external imagery—like the earlier Spyders—save for a small, round emblem on the deck lid. The chin spoiler was a standard Corsa feature in 1966.

from either a frugal 90 horsepower 153 cubic inch four-cylinder or a 120 horsepower 194 cubic inch six. Although a V-8 swap was made available midyear as a dealer option, its price tag ran as high as 75 percent of a 1962 Nova sports coupe's sticker.

Performance imagery came along in 1963 with the Super Sport option. First offered on Impalas in 1961, the SS package for Novas included special trim and wheel covers, bucket seats, instrumentation, and a deluxe steering wheel. True performance debuted in 1964 with the first optional Chevy II V-8, the 195 horsepower 283. Two years later, Chevrolet's little Nova joined super car ranks with the addition of the L79 option, a 350 horsepower 327 that transformed a Chevy II into a polite 15.10 second quarter-mile contender.

Small-blocks were the limit for Chevy II customers until 1968, when the 396 big-block

became available early in the model run. Standard power for the 1968 Nova SS 396 came from a somewhat mild 350 horsepower big-block, with a serious 375-horse version also listed. According to *Popular Hot Rodding*, a 375 horsepower SS 396 Nova could run the quarter in 13.85 seconds, topping out at 104mph. SS 396 Novas were dropped after 1970, leaving the 270 horsepower 350 cubic inch small-block as the top power choice in 1971.

A revised turbocharger and an increase in displacement from 145 cubic inches to 164 cubic inches helped pump up output from the Spyder's 150 horsepower to 180 horsepower in 1965. Here, a Saginaw four-speed sends this 1966 turbo six's torque through a 3.55:1 positraction transaxle.

With bucket seats, a four-speed stick, and an attractive dash layout featuring full instrumentation, a turbocharged 1966 Corsa Corvair offered as much sporty imagery inside as it did performance beneath its rear deck lid.

Right
A Nova SS convertible was offered only in 1963, the same year the Super Sport equipment was first made available to Chevy II buyers. Six-cylinder power was as hot as it got for the 1963 Nova SS, though an ultra-expensive (roughly $1500 or more) dealer-option V-8 swap was listed. Super Sport Nova production for 1963 reached 42,432, with no breakdown given for sports coupe or convertible. The 1963 Nova Super Sport's exterior features included SS wheel covers (from the 1963 Impala Super Sport), special beltline trim, "Nova SS" emblems on the tail and rear quarters, and a silver rear coverpanel.

Priced at $161, the Super Sport option for the 1963 Chevy II Nova added bucket seats, a deluxe sport steering wheel, and a four-gauge (oil, ammeter, temperature, fuel) instrument cluster. A bright molding spanned the center of the dash, and a "Nova SS" emblem was added to the glovebox. Powerglide-equipped Nova Super Sports got a floor shifter with an attractive chrome plate (all three-speed cars included column shifts).

Right
The Chevy II's body was restyled in 1966, while the Nova SS was recharged with the addition of the optional L79 327 V-8. Featuring a Holley carburetor, 11:1 compression, and big-valve heads, the L79 produced 350 horsepower. Sadly, the L79 option was discontinued for 1967, the year in which front disc brakes were first offered. This yellow 1967 Nova SS shows off its attractive, slotted Rally wheels, which were included when front discs were ordered.

Nova SS: a quick looking coupe you can order with the toughest block on the block.
—1968 Chevrolet advertisement

Like Chevelle SS 396s, a big-block Nova Super Sport featured a blacked-out rear cove panel with an "SS" badge in the center. An "SS" steering wheel was also included inside. This gold 1969 SS 396 Nova is one of 5,262 equipped with the 375 horsepower big-block; another 1,947 were built with the 350 horsepower 396. Total 1969 Nova Super Sport production, including small-blocks, was 17,654.

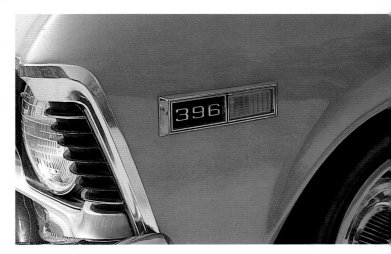

This innocuous badge incorporated into the side-marker light on both front fenders was the only clue to the presence of a 1969 SS 396 Nova. Priced at $280 above the cost of a Nova coupe, the standard Super Sport featured a 350 cubic inch small-block V-8. Price for the 350 horsepower SS 396 package was $464; the 375 horsepower version cost $596.

Left
Fitted with 11:1 compression, a big Holley four-barrel on an aluminum intake, free-breathing heads, and solid lifters, the 375 horsepower 396 was a no-nonsense muscular powerplant, "a very serious engine to stuff into an unsuspecting Chevy II," according to *Car and Driver.* Performance was equally serious at 14.5 seconds through the quarter-mile. Top speed was an estimated 121mph.

Chapter 3

Mid-Sized Muscle
From Chevelle to Monte Carlo

Chevrolet general manager Semon E. "Bunkie" Knudsen introduced the Chevelle in August 1964 to rave reviews, both from the press and from the car-buying public. Chevy's popular new A-body was smart looking, easy to handle, and offered ample comfort. Performance potential was also present, though it would be more than a year before that was fully tapped.

Initially, the best a performance-minded Chevelle customer could do was to add the $162 Super Sport equipment group, which featured more sporty flair than anything else. Even mundane six-cylinder power was a Super Sport option in 1964 and 1965; but midway through the 1964 model year, the 327 cubic inch small-block V-8 was made available. Then in 1965 the truly hot 350 horsepower L79 327 appeared as an option.

Really big news came in February 1965 when Knudsen again did the introductory honors, this time for Chevy's first SS 396 Chevelle, the fabled 1965 Z16. The limited edition Z16 was powered by a 375 horsepower 396 mated to a Muncie four-speed and loaded with a host of options that ran its bottom line up to about $4,200. Publicity was the driving force behind the Z16's existence. Only 201 examples were built—200 hardtops and one mysterious convertible. The lone drop-top was built as an executive car. It was eventually sold off, and its final fate remains unknown to date.

Credit for inspiring COPO 9562 Chevelle production basically goes to Don Yenko, who ordered ninety-nine 427-equipped A-bodies for his Chevy dealership in Canonsburg, Pennsylvania. When the Chevelles arrived, they were converted into Yenko Super Cars. Graphics and badges identical to the Yenko Camaro's were added, as were optional Atlas five-spoke mags on request. Of the ninety-nine 1969 Yenko Chevelle SCs built, twenty-two were four-speed cars, and seventy-seven were equipped with Turbo-Hydramatics, like this Fathom Green example.

After 1965, Chev elle Super Sports came only with the 396 cubic inch Mk IV V-8—no more small-blocks or six-cylinders. Offered in more affordable, less plush form, the base 1966 SS 396 Chevelle relied on a 325 horsepower 396, with 360- and 375-horse big-blocks available at extra cost. Carrying a price tag right around $3,000, Chevrolet's SS 396 quickly raced to the forefront of Detroit's super car scene.

In 1969, the SS 396 package was improved greatly with the addition of front disc brakes and the F41 sport suspension group as standard equipment. As for power options, new for 1969 was the aluminum head L89 option for the L78 375 horsepower 396, features that didn't change output on the street, but saved considerable weight at the track. Also new was the COPO 9562 Chevelle, a rare 427-powered variant created in order to supply Don Yenko

With its 115in wheelbase (identical to the 1955 Chevy), super clean slab sides, and scalloped rear wheel openings, Chevrolet's 1964 Chevelle clearly picked up where the famed "Hot One" had left off. The crossflag fender emblem on this 1964 Chevelle Super Sport indicates the presence of the optional 327 cubic inch V-8, introduced in three power levels midway through the model year. The L30 327 was rated at 250 horsepower, while the L74 put out 300 horses. At the top was the mysterious 365 horsepower L76 Corvette 327, a true performance powerplant that was officially offered then quickly cancelled before true production got underway. No more than a handful were built; this 1964 SS was assembled to L76 specs by its owner to demonstrate an ultra-rare breed.

141

The Super Sport option group for the 1964 Chevelle was identified by special trim on the upper body line, rockers, and wheel openings; SS wheel covers; and "SS" badges on the rear quarters and back cove panel. Super Sport Chevelle hardtop production for 1964 was 57,445 for V-8 cars and 8,224 for six-cylinders. Standard power for a V-8 Chevelle SS in 1964 was a 195 horsepower 283 cubic inch small-block.

with base models for his Yenko Super Car transformations.

Once GM's 400 cubic inch limit for intermediates was lifted after 1969, the sky became the limit. Chevy's SS 396 remained available—with actual displacement at 402 cubic inches. But the top dog was the SS 454, available in two forms—the 360 horsepower LS5 and the

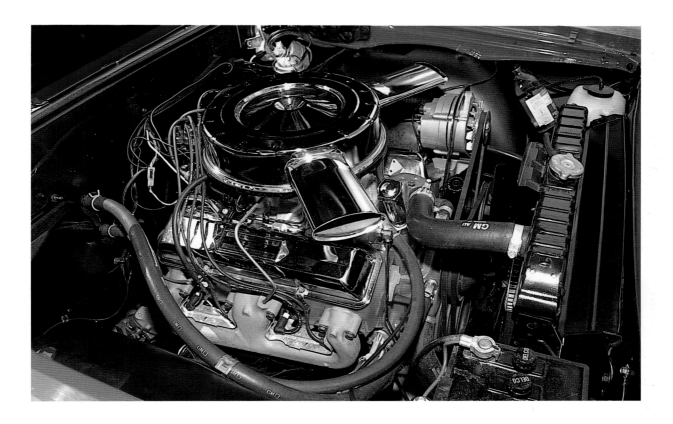

450 horsepower LS6. The latter engine's greater horsepower was attributable in part to closed chamber heads with bigger valves, 11.25:1 compression, a 0.520in lift cam, and a 780cfm Holley four-barrel. Able to leap tall buildings in a single bound, the 13-second LS6 ranks as one of the greatest super cars of all time. But the LS6 legend was short-lived. Although initially offered again, this time in 425 horsepower tune, the LS6 454 Chevelle failed to reappear in 1971, a victim of skyrocketing insurance rates, growing safety concerns, and impinging emissions standards.

By 1971, the Chevelle SS was again made available, though now with small-block power

Reportedly the A-body chassis made it difficult to equip the 365 horsepower L76 327 with large enough exhaust manifolds, which helped kill the project before it ever got off the ground. A certified street killer, the L76 small-block featured a solid-lifter "special performance cam," 11:1 compression, a big four-barrel carb on an aluminum intake, and a dual-snorkel air cleaner. According to rumors, a prototype L76 Chevelle ran 0–60mph in six seconds.

for the first time since 1965. The SS 454 managed to stick around through 1972, still a force to be reckoned with, but only a mere shadow of its former self. After 1973, all that remained were memories.

Z16 Chevelles differed from 1965 small-block Super Sports in back, where the "Malibu SS" rear quarter script was removed (reinstalled up front) and the tail dechromed. Less ornate 300 series taillights were installed, as was a blacked-out rear cove panel and a "Malibu SS 396" deck lid badge. A base 1965 V-8 Chevelle SS was priced at $2,600. Throw in the $1,501.05 for RPO Z16, along with the cost of a few other options, and the overall sticker got heavy in a hurry.

Left
A limited edition, fully loaded teaser for the big-block Chevelle bloodline to come, 1965's Z16 was both high-priced and high-powered. All 201 Z16s were equipped with the 375 horsepower 396 cubic inch Mk IV V-8 backed by a Muncie M20 four-speed with 2.56:1 low—an automatic transmission wasn't available. Gold-line rubber with simulated mag-style wheel covers, a blacked-out grille, "396 Turbo-Jet" fender emblems, and the transplanted "Malibu SS" badge (from the rear quarters to the front fenders) were all included in the Z16 deal.

145

Appearing first in 427 cubic inch "Mystery Motor" form at the Daytona 500 in February 1963, Chevrolet's Mk IV big-block V-8, RPO L37, was introduced for street duty in 1965. The 396 cubic inch mill became an option for Corvettes and full-sized models and was made the heart of RPO Z16. Under Z16 Chevelle hoods, the L37 396 was rated at 375 horsepower. Unlike the 425 horsepower Corvette 396, which used a solid-lifter cam, the Chevelle big-block relied on hydraulic lifters. Other L37 features included a Holley four-barrel, aluminum intake, and 11:1 extruded aluminum pistons.

Standard 1965 Z16 interior included bucket seats, front and rear seatbelts, AM/FM four-speaker stereo, a 160mph speedometer, 6000rpm tach, oil gauge, and dash-mounted clock. Optional equipment seen here includes power windows and a sport steering wheel with simulated woodgrain rim. As with exterior paint, Z16 interior color choices numbered only three: black, white and red, with red not offered with the Crocus Yellow paint. Regal Red and Tuxedo Black finishes were the other two exterior choices.

Chevelle SS396. And the SS doesn't stand for "Standing Still."

—1967 Chevrolet advertisement

147

This cowl plenum intake system was offered over dealers' parts counters for 1966 Chevelle SS 396s (the setup had first appeared on the rare 1963 Z11 A/FX Impala), though it would become better known as a Z/28 Camaro option the following year. A rare Chevelle feature, this NASCAR-style induction setup sits atop a 375 horsepower L78 396, of which 3,099 found their way under SS 396 hoods in 1966. Also featured on this car is the M22 Muncie "Rock Crusher" four-speed, one of only eighteen ordered by 1966 SS 396 buyers.

Right
For one year only, the SS 396 package, RPO Z25, was offered on both the top-line Malibu hardtops and convertibles, and on the lower priced 300 series models, making an SS 396 sedan possible in 1969. No breakdowns are available, but this Hugger Orange SS 396 300 Deluxe sedan is certainly a rare bird, especially when you consider it's powered by an aluminum-head L89 396. All 1969 SS 396s, regardless of body style or model line, came with 14x7in five-spoke sport wheels.

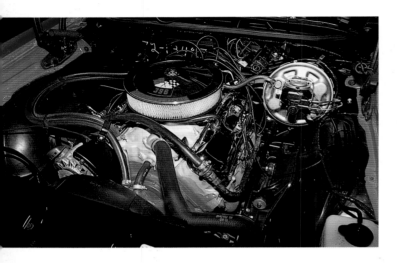

Aimed at racers who preferred cutting weight wherever possible, RPO L89 added a pair of lightweight aluminum cylinder heads to the 375 horsepower L78 396. Output for the L89/L78 big-block V-8 remained the same. Only 400 L89 Super Sport Chevelles were built for 1969, with estimates claiming as many as six of the aluminum-head 396s installed in SS 396 300 Deluxe sedans.

The 425 horsepower L72 427 carried no identification under a COPO Chevelle's hood, leaving some believing it was just another 396. Much hotter than even the 375 horsepower L78, the L72 featured 11:1 compression, a 0.520in lift, solid-lifter cam, and an 800cfm Holley four-barrel carb. COPO Chevelles turned low 13 second quarter-miles. Although exact production figures aren't available, it is known that Chevrolet built ninety-six L72 V-8s for COPO Chevelles with Turbo-Hydramatics (code MP) and another 277 425 horsepower 427s for four-speed COPO 9562 applications. The 373 total represents engines built, not cars assembled.

Right
Somewhat of a mystery still today, the 1969 COPO 9562 Chevelle was a little-known variation on the big-block A-body theme. Like the COPO Camaros, this Chevelle was equipped with the L72 427 Corvette V-8. COPO Chevelles featured the SS 396's hood, exhaust extensions, grille, and blacked-out tail treatment (with "SS 396" badges removed front and rear), but the car wasn't a Super Sport. Both the SS 396 bodyside stripes and Rally wheels were optional, with the Rallys being 15x7in units; optional Malibu Rally rims in 1969 were fourteen-inchers, while all SS 396s rolled on their own exclusive 14x7in five-spoke wheels.

The L72 427 under Yenko Chevelle hoods was rated at 450 horsepower. A set of Doug Thorley headers was offered as a Yenko option, but few were ordered. According to *Super Stock & Drag Illustrated's* Ro McGonegal, a 1969 Yenko Chevelle could trip the lights at the far end of the quarter-mile in 13.31 seconds at 108mph—on street tires.

Right
Considered by many as the king of the muscle car hill, the 1970 LS6 SS 454 Chevelle ranked easily among Detroit's quickest performance machines, achieving low 13-second quarter-miles with relative ease. Breaking into the 12-second bracket was also possible with a few modifications. This LS6 convertible, looking somewhat plain without the typical cowl induction hood and optional striping, is one of about twenty built (some production estimates also go as high as seventy-five). Total 1970 LS6 production—convertible, hardtop, and El Camino—was 4,475.

Left
Car Life claimed the 450 horsepower LS6 454 was "the best super car engine ever released by General Motors." Free-breathing, closed-chamber heads; 11.25:1 compression; a 0.520in lift, solid-lifter cam; and a 780cfm Holley four-barrel atop a low-rise aluminum manifold were among the LS6's supporting cast. Torque output was an impressive 500lb-ft at 4000rpm. The twin-snorkel air cleaner shown here is one of three types used on LS6 454 Chevelles.

Previous pages
From 1966 on, El Camino models could be equipped with nearly all features common to Chevelle Super Sports—including the 396 big-block V-8. It wasn't until 1968, however, that they actually wore Super Sport badges . For 1968 only, the SS 396 El Camino was a separate model in itself. From 1969 to 1970, the SS 396 package, RPO Z25, was listed as an option for El Caminos, as it was in Chevelle ranks. In 1971, the SS 396's RPO number changed to Z15. This 1970 SS 396 El Camino is equipped with the popular optional cowl induction hood and 350 horsepower big-block.

Above
Joining Chevrolet's A-body ranks in 1970 was the Monte Carlo, a personal luxury car that could also be outfitted in Super Sport garb. Offered in both 1970 and 1971, the SS 454 Monte Carlo was a classy torque monster fit with heavy-duty suspension. Exterior identification consisted only of two small "SS 454" rocker badges and twin chrome exhaust extensions in back. This 1970 Monte Carlo SS 454 is one of 3,823 built; another 1,919 rolled out in 1971.

**Standard power for the 1970 SS 454 Monte Carlo
was the Chevelle's 360 horsepower LS5 454.
Compression was 10.25:1 and maximum torque
was 500lb-ft at 3200rpm.**

Chapter 4

A Breed Above
Camaro: Chevrolet's Pony Car

In August 1964, General Motors officials gave the go-ahead for the F-car project, Chevrolet's response to Ford's pony car progenitor, the Mustang. Chevy's F-body Camaro, introduced on September 29, 1966, hit the ground running, making up more than two years of lost time in short order.

Initially, the hot Camaro package featured the ever-present Super Sport option group, which included the 295 horsepower 350 cubic inch small-block, a special hood with simulated air intakes, an accent stripe on the nose, SS badging, and wide-oval red-stripe rubber. The original Camaro SS was a certified eye-catcher, but no match for Ford's potent big-block GT Mustang. Chevrolet solved this problem in November 1966 when the big-block 396 Mk IV V-8 was made an optional Super Sport power source—first in 325 horsepower trim, followed later by the 375 horsepower L78 version.

Yet another impressive introduction came in November 1966, this one for the legendary Z/28, intended to homologate the Camaro platform for competition in Sports Car Club of America (SCCA) Trans-Am competition. The Z/28's 302 cubic inch V-8, one of Detroit's hottest small-blocks, was created by installing the 283's crankshaft in a 327 block. This ploy allowed Chevy to stay within SCCA racing's 305 cubic inch legal limit. Conservatively rated at 290 horsepower, Chevy's hybrid small-block was described by *Car and Driver* as "the most responsive American V-8 we've ever tested."

A revised accent stripe up front represented the most noticeable Camaro SS change for 1968. Rally Sport options for 1968 totaled 40,977; Super Sport production was 27,884. Note the restyled Rally wheel with its large center cap, again a feature included with the optional front disc brakes. In 1968, SS 396 Camaro buyers could choose from three big-block V-8s, as the 325 horsepower and 375 horsepower 396s were joined by a 350 horsepower version.

The 302 would remain the heart and soul of the Z/28 through 1969.

F-body news for 1968 included recognizable exterior emblems for the Z/28 and two additional 396 big-blocks. The 350 horsepower 396 joined the 325- and 375-horse versions on the SS equipment list, as did the rarely seen L89 aluminum head option for the L78 396. Retaining the L78's 375 horsepower rating, the L89 option simply lightened the load for race-minded customers.

Revised sheet metal helped make the

Priced at $210, the Super Sport package for the 1967 Camaro featured a distinctive accent stripe up front, fake air inlets on the hood, "SS" badging, and a 295 horsepower 350 cubic inch small-block V-8. Later in the year, the nose stripe would become an option for all Camaros. This 1967 SS convertible also features the Rally Sport equipment group, which added hideaway headlights. The mag-style wheel covers were optional. Camaro SS production for 1967, coupes and convertibles, totaled 34,411. RS convertibles numbered 10,675.

exceptionally stylish 1969 Camaro perhaps the most popular edition of Chevy's long-running F-body pony car performance package. Power options were basically unchanged with one major exception—the exotic ZL1 427. Featuring an aluminum block and heads, the race-ready ZL1 was created using the Central Office Production Order system, a quick way to cut corporate red tape, as well as avoid upper office roadblocks. COPO ZL1 Camaros were brutally fast, scorching the quarter-mile in nearly 13 seconds flat. Chevy performance guru Vince Piggins and Illinois Chevrolet dealer Fred Gibb put their heads together and used COPOs to build fifty ZL1 Camaros for Gibbs' lot in La Harpe, Illinois. Another nineteen COPO 9560 ZL1 Camaros were built for various other dealers across the country.

Another Chevy dealer, Don Yenko of Canonsburg, Pennsylvania, turned to Piggins and his COPO pipeline in 1969 to supply Yenko Chevrolet with factory-built 427 Camaros which he would then convert into Yenko Super Cars. Listed under COPO 9561, the L72 425 horsepower cast-iron 427 Camaro became the base for the 1969 Yenko Camaro, a high-powered hybrid capable of low 13-second quarters.

A stunning restyle shaped the Camaro image for 1970. For the first time, the Z/28 package was not powered by the 302, a variation of the Corvette's hot 360 horsepower LT1 350 cubic inch small-block taking its place. More of an off-the-line warrior, the 1970-1/2 Z/28 offered quarter-mile performance in the low 14-second range.

Listed under RPO L48, the Camaro Super Sport's 295 horsepower 350 featured 10.25:1 compression, hydraulic lifters, and forged steel rods and crank. With a few minor tuning tricks, courtesy of performance dealer Bill Thomas, *Hot Rod* managed a best quarter-mile run of 14.85 seconds at 95.65mph in a 1967 L48 SS Camaro. *Car and Driver's* results were considerably slower at 16.1 seconds 87mph.

A good ZL-1 . . . would produce somewhere in excess of 500hp without any attention to detail whatsoever.
—Tom Langdon in *Chevrolet Big-Block Muscle Cars*

Left
The SS package's price jumped to $263 when the L35 325 horsepower 396 big-block was announced as a Camaro Super Sport power choice early in the 1967 model run. The attractive Rally wheels on this Rally Sport SS 396 Camaro signify the presence of the optional front disc brakes. The vented 14in Rally rims were included with the RPO J52 front discs.

Rated at 325 horsepower, RPO L35 was the base 396 big-block for the 1967 SS Camaro. The hotter 375 horsepower L78 396 waited in the wings, but the cost of admission was nearly double that of the L35. The impressive 375 horsepower 396 featured a durable four-bolt main bearing block, while the 325 horsepower L35 had two-bolt mains.

Left
Fifteen-inch Corvette Rally rims and contrasting hood stripes represented the only exterior identification for Chevrolet's first Z/28 Camaro, introduced November 29, 1966, at Riverside International Raceway in California. The legendary Z/28 fender badges wouldn't come until March 1968. Z/28 equipment included front disc brakes, F41 sport suspension, quick-ratio steering, 3.73:1 gears, a Muncie four-speed, and the sensational 302 cubic inch small-block. Only 602 Z/28s were built for 1967.

The Z/28's hybrid 302 was conservatively rated at 290 horsepower and featured 11:1 compression, a hot solid-lifter cam, L79 327 heads with big valves, transistorized ignition, and an 800cfm Holley four-barrel on an aluminum intake. Modeled after NASCAR racing induction tricks designed by Smokey Yunick, the cowl induction air cleaner was a $79 option delivered in a Z/28's trunk to be installed by the dealer.

Previous pages

Chevy performance proponent Vince Piggins first suggested building the Z/28 in August 1966 to homologate the package for SCCA Trans-Am competition, where Mustangs and Plymouth Barracudas would be the Camaro's main rivals. Piggins' first choice for the car's name was "Cheetah," but in the end it was the optional group's RPO number that got the nod. Little known in its first year, the Z/28 jumped considerably in popularity for 1968, reaching sales of 7,199, followed by 19,014 in 1969.

Although the Z/28 Camaro was better suited for race action at the track, it could be equipped with all Camaro luxury and convenience options, including the Rally Sport package with its hideaway headlights. Here, this uncommonly plush 1967 Z/28 interior includes optional deluxe Parchment appointments, the sporty center console and gauge cluster.

With solid lifters and 11:1 compression, the L78 375 horsepower 396 was clearly meant for some serious action. When backed by a Muncie four-speed and 3.31:1 positraction gears, an L78 SS 396 Camaro could easily run the quarter-mile in the 14-second range. Special-duty differentials with stump-pulling ratios like 4.10:1, 4.56:1, and 4.88:1 promised even more.

Left
Race-minded Chevy dealer Don Yenko first began transplanting 427s into Camaros at his Canonsburg, Pennsylvania, facility in 1967. In 1969, he ordered a special run of COPO 9561 F-bodies—Camaros equipped with 425 horsepower Corvette 427s. Distinctive Yenko graphics and badges, 427 emblems, and a choice between the standard COPO equipment 15in Rally rims or optional Atlas five-spoke mags were part of the Yenko package.

Although some minor confusion exists concerning exactly how many 1969 Yenko Camaro SCs were built, the widely accepted—and presently documented—figure is 201. COPO 9561 L72 Camaros were also sold by Chevrolet, with 1,015 425 horsepower 427 V-8s produced for F-body applications in 1969. The ZL2 air induction hood was a standard COPO 9561 feature, while the "Yenko/SC" striping and 427 badges were installed at Canonsburg. This SC's vinyl roof was a factory option.

171

The big news isn't the gauges . . . it's what the gauges are connected to!

—1966 Chevrolet advertisement

The L72 427 lurking beneath a Yenko Camaro hood featured a cast-iron block and heads and an advertised 450 horsepower. An 800cfm Holley four-barrel fed the beast, a solid-lifter cam helped deliver the juice, and 11:1 pistons squeezed the mixture. Backed by an M21 Muncie four-speed and standard 4.10:1 positraction gears, the L72 transformed a Camaro into a quarter-mile terror— 12.80 at 108mph off the lot with street rubber and optional Doug Thorley headers, according to *Super Stock & Drag Illustrated's* Ro McGonegal. Slicks and tuning tricks lowered those figures even further to an astonishing 12.10 seconds at 114mph.

All 1969 Yenko models, Camaro or Chevelle, got custom headrest covers featuring the "sYc" logo for Yenko Super Car. Joining the 201 Yenko Camaros in 1969 were another ninety-nine similarly bedecked 427 Yenko Chevelle SCs.

Conservatively rated at 430 horsepower, the 12:1 compression ZL1 427 easily put out more than 500 horses, demonstrated by its ability to run the quarter in nearly 13 seconds flat. ZL1 427 features included an iron-sleeved aluminum block and open chamber aluminum heads, along with an aluminum bellhousing and transmission case. These helped keep engine weight down in the 500 pound range; a ZL1 big-block weighed no more than a small-block V-8.

Right
Other than the ZL2 air induction hood, no exterior clues give away the identity of an awesome 1969 ZL1 427 COPO 9560 Camaro. Along with that hood and the 430 horsepower all-aluminum 427, COPO 9560 equipment also included a heavy-duty Harrison radiator, transistorized ignition, special suspension, and a 14-bolt rear end. Mandatory options included front disc brakes and a choice between M21 or M22 "Rock Crusher" Muncie four-speeds and the Turbo-Hydramatic 400 automatic. Typical ZL1 stickered at nearly $7,300. Only sixty-nine were built.

174

Chapter 5

America's Sports Car
Classic Corvettes

Forty years and a million models after it first set rubber on American roads, Chevrolet's Corvette remains as this country's premier sports car. This achievement shouldn't be dimmed by the fact that it has basically reigned for four decades as this country's *only* sports car. Pretenders to the throne have been few, and save for Carroll Shelby's uncivilized Cobra, itself a match only as far as sheer brute force was concerned, the Corvette has remained unequalled .

Beginnings, however, were humble. The first-edition 1953–1955 Corvette was somewhat awkward and weakly-received; the public considered it more of a curiosity than anything. Insufficient market interest almost cancelled Harley Earl's 'glass-bodied baby in 1954, but V-8 power saved it the following year. Zora Arkus-Duntov's growing involvement with the car also helped to turn things around. By 1956 Chevrolet had itself a winner. A startling restyle, combined with some serious performance engineering courtesy of Duntov, put the 1956 Corvette on the right track. Armed with two four-barrel carburetors, the 1955 Corvette's polite 265 cubic inch V-8 was transformed into 1956's 255 horsepower bully.

Fuel injection debuted in 1957, landing the Corvette's enlarged 283 cubic inch small-block into the newly created "one-horsepower-per-cubic-inch" club (Chrysler had broken the barrier the year before with the 300B's 355 horsepower 354 cubic inch hemi). Although early

Optional side exhausts and standard four-wheel disc brakes debuted in 1965, but the really big news came up front in the form of the Corvette's first big-block, the 396 cubic inch Mk IV V-8. The 396 Mk IV, nicknamed "porcupine head" for its canted-valve design, was a direct descendant of the 427 cubic inch Mk II engine that shook the NASCAR troops at Daytona just as GM was closing the door on factory racing activities in February 1963. A special bulging hood was included when the 396 Turbo-Jet was ordered.

Chevrolet's fiberglass Corvette two-seater was offered only in Polo White when introduced in 1953. Three additional shades were added in 1954: Pennant Blue, Sportsman Red, and black. In all, 3,640 1954 Corvettes were built, less than one-third of Chevy's projected total. Opinions varied concerning styling and performance. But even though the car's creator, Zora Arkus-Duntov, wasn't happy with the 1953–1954 Corvette's performance, handling and acceleration were above average by American standards of the time; 0–60mph took 11 seconds, and the car topped out at 105mph.

versions of the injected V-8 were often disagreeable and difficult to maintain, it would remain as the top Corvette performance option through 1965. The 327 was the last fuel-injected Corvette engine of the 1960s, achieving a maximum output rating of 375 horsepower before it was displaced by the brutish 396 cubic inch Mk IV big-block V-8 in 1966.

Partial restyles in 1958 and 1960 freshened the Corvette's face, but paled in comparison to 1963's makeover. The body was Bill Mitchell's idea, with final lines penned by Larry Shinoda. Looking an awful lot like Mitchell's Stingray racer of 1959, the all-new Corvette Sting Ray was as innovative underneath as it was stunning on top, thanks to Duntov's devotion to

Powering the 1953, 1954, and early 1955 Corvettes was Chevrolet's 235 cubic inch Blue Flame six-cylinder, based on the same "Stovebolt" six that served more mundane duty under standard passenger car hoods. As a Corvette powerplant, the 235 six featured three Carter carbs, a relatively radical high-lift cam, 8:1 compression, and a split exhaust manifold feeding dual exhausts. Maximum output was 150 horsepower at 4200rpm. This 1954 Blue Flame six uses twin air cleaners in place of the three "bullet-type" breathers installed in 1953. Complete chrome dress-up was also available for these engines.

Looking much sleeker, the second-generation 1956–1957 Corvette was not only more popular than its predecessor but also more civilized, with the addition of roll-up windows and a removable hardtop. Performance improvements included various chassis updates to improve handling and optional twin four-barrel carburetors in 1956, followed by fuel injection in 1957. This black beauty is one of 6,339 Corvettes built for 1957; 1956 production was 3,467.

independent rear suspension. In reference to the 1963 Sting Ray, Duntov told *Car and Driver*, "I now have a Corvette I can be proud to drive in Europe." Offered both as Corvette's first coupe rendition, as well as in typical topless fashion, Shinoda's timeless Sting Ray shape lasted through five model runs, and many feel the Corvette was never better.

Performance enhancements during the span included the aforementioned big-block introduction for 1965, a powerful package that was pumped up to 427 cubic inches in 1966. The awesome aluminum head L88 option for the 427 appeared in 1967, followed by the

In 1957, engineers bored out the Corvette's small-block V-8 to 283 cubic inches and upped the output ante to one horsepower per cubic inch with the optional Ramjet fuel injection setup. Actually, the Ramjet option was available in two forms, the 283 horsepower version with 10.5:1 compression and the 250 horsepower 283 fuelie with a 9.5:1 ratio. Also new for 1957 was a four-speed manual transmission. According to *Road & Track*, a four-speed 283 horsepower fuelie Corvette could go 0–60mph in 5.7 seconds. Quarter-mile time for the same car was a sizzling 14.3 seconds.

ultimate big-block Vette, 1969's all-aluminum 427 ZL1.

Meanwhile, Mitchell and Shinoda had turned out another new Corvette look for 1968. Featuring what would become General Motors' familiar "Coke-bottle" body, the fifth generation Corvette was, in *Car and Driver*'s opinion, "the best yet."

In 1970, the optional 370 horsepower LT1 350 cubic inch V-8 appeared, balancing the brutish big-block boulevard Vettes—which had reached their pinnacle that same year in LS5 454 cubic inch form—with a well-rounded agile road rocket. Not since the fuel-injected 327 had disappeared after 1965 had Corvette buyers been able to combine serious small-block power with a well-balanced, road-hugging stance. The LT1 small-block and 454 big-block carried the Corvette banner high into Detroit's post-performance years—the LT1 falling by the wayside after 1972, and the 454 doing the same two years later.

Left
The last of the solid-axle Corvettes, the 1962 model foretold the coming of the classic Sting Ray in 1963 through its boat-tail rear, which had first appeared in 1961. Although its grille was devoid of the earlier models' teeth, the 1962 Corvette's quad headlight front end was a direct descendant of the design introduced for 1958. Top performance option in 1962 was the 360 horsepower fuel-injected 327 cubic inch V-8. Total 1962 Corvette production was 14,531.

The Corvette's 283 cubic inch V-8 was bored and stroked to 327 cubic inches for 1962. In basic tune, the 1962 Corvette 327 was rated at 250 horsepower. Three other 327s were available, the 300- and 340-horse carbureted small-blocks and the king-of-the-hill 360 horsepower fuel-injected version.

Sports cars are by their nature controversial: they arouse the interest of the adolescent— and of those reaching second childhood.

—Roy Lunn, SAE paper 611F in *American Muscle*

Befitting its name, the totally restyled 1963 Corvette Sting Ray featured its own "stinger," a spine that ran the length of the car; it began as a center bulge on the hood, and ended in this split window design on the coupe model's boat-tail rear. Duntov didn't like the idea, nor did drivers who preferred seeing what they were about to back over. But Bill Mitchell insisted the split window theme remain, which it did for one year only.

A serious performance powerplant with solid lifters and 11:1 compression, the 1965 Corvette's 396 Turbo-Jet produced maximum power of 425 horsepower at 6400rpm. Maximum torque was 415lb-ft at 4000rpm. All this brute force translated into a 0–60mph time of 5.7 seconds and quarter-mile performance of 14.1 seconds at 103mph. Reported top end for a 1965 396 Corvette was 136mph.

Left

In 1966, the 396 Turbo-Jet became the 427 Turbo-Jet, available in 390- and 425-horse forms. A triple-carb option in 1967 pumped up output to 435 horsepower, but the most potent Corvette power choice that year was actually advertised at five fewer horses. Given a 430 horsepower factory rating, the rare L88 427 probably put out somewhere between 500 and 600 real horses. Only 20 L88 Corvettes were produced for 1967.

Obviously built for racing, L88 427 features included aluminum heads, beefy internals, a 0.540/0.560 solid-lifter cam, 12.5:1 compression, a huge 830cfm Holley four-barrel, and an open-element air cleaner. Knowing a racer would quickly replace it anyway, the L88's exhaust system remained typical stock Corvette hardware. Backing up the L88 was a 10.5in heavy-duty clutch and a lightweight nodular iron flywheel.

In 1969, the awesome L88 Corvette was superseded by the outrageous ZL1, an all-aluminum 427 also laughably rated at 430 horsepower. Again, actual output was more like 560 horsepower, but who was counting? Factory numbers games mattered little once behind the wheel of a ZL1 Corvette. Press tests put performance at a shocking 12.1 seconds through the quarter-mile, topping out at 116mph. Of course, that much speed didn't come cheap; the ZL1 option cost around $3,000. Only two were built.

Weighing some 100lb less than the aluminum-head L88, the ZL1 kept its weight down by using an iron-sleeved aluminum cylinder block. Everything the L88 was, the ZL1 did one better. Internals were even beefier, and a modified solid-lifter cam featuring revised ramp profiles was included, as were big-valve, open chamber aluminum cylinder heads. Compression remained the same, but pistons were reinforced.

In contrast to the brutal big-block Corvettes, the LT1-equipped models, introduced in 1970, were well-balanced performers; agile as well as muscular, they took many enthusiasts back to the fuelie's days when Corvettes were more sports car and less quarter-mile warrior. For 1970, the hot 350 cubic inch LT1 small-block was rated at 370 horsepower. In 1971 that rating dropped to 330 horsepower, and the final rendition was advertised at 255 net horses. This 1972 LT1 Corvette is one of 1,741 built. Production in 1970 and 1971 was 1,287 and 1,949, respectively. All LT1s got a distinctive hood modeled after the 1968–1969 L88/ZL1 design.

DODGE/PLYMOUTH
MUSCLE CARS

You know what a Hemi is. Its got valves as big as stove lids. A plug jammed right in the middle of the combustion chamber. 426 cubes. And a thermal efficiency that is making a lot of people see red . . . taillights.

—*Dodge advertisement,* 1964

Acknowledgments

Many thanks go out to all the people who took the time to share their magnificent Mopars with the readers of this book. In order of appearance, they are:

George Shelley, Pompano Beach, Florida: Chrysler 300C convertible; Marvin and Joan Hughes, Ocala, Florida: 1957 Dodge D500 convertible; Gary Ogletree, Fayetteville, Georgia: 1958 Plymouth Fury; Ken Lanious, Forest Park, Illinois: 1959 Plymouth Sport Fury; Doug West, Preston, Idaho: 1959 DeSoto Adventurer; Paul Garlick, Lehigh Acres, Florida: 1961 Dodge Polara D500 convertible; Dan Heller, Tolono, Illinois: 1964 Chrysler 300K; Dennis Haak, Annville, Pennsylvania: 1960 Dodge Dart Phoenix D500; John Buxman, Eustis, Florida: 1962 Dodge Polara 413 Max Wedge; Bill and Barbara Jacobsen, Silver Dollar Classic Cars, Odessa: Florida, 1963 Dodge 330 426 Max Wedge; Steve Conti, St. Petersburg, Florida: 1969 Dodge Dart GTS; Garrett Bates, Pompano Beach, Florida: 1971 Dodge Demon; Bernie and Sheila Hage, Tampa, Florida: 1972 Plymouth Duster; Marvin and Joan Hughes, Ocala, Florida: 1966 Plymouth Belvedere II 426 Hemi; Roger and Janet Dunkelmann, Palm Beach Gardens, Florida: 1966 Dodge Charger 426 Hemi; Tony George, Clearwater, Florida: 1967 Plymouth GTX; Floyd Garrett, Fernandina Beach, Florida: 1968 Plymouth Road Runner 426 Hemi; Stuart Echolls, Lakeland, Florida: 1969 Dodge Super Bee 440 Six Pack; Bill and Barbara Jacobsen, Silver Dollar Classic Cars, Odessa, Florida: 1969 Dodge Daytona, 1969 Dodge Charger 500 426 Hemi, and 1970 Plymouth Superbird 426 Hemi; Steve Siegel, Lakeland, Florida: 1971 Dodge Charger R/T 426 Hemi; Jim Ludera, Bradenton, Florida: 1970 Plymouth Hemi 'Cuda; Robert Yappell, Princeton, Florida: 1970 Dodge T/A Challenger; Bill and Barbara Jacobsen, Silver Dollar Classic Cars, Odessa, Florida: 1970 Plymouth 'Cuda 440+6 and 1971 Dodge Challenger convertible.

ROAD RUNNER

SUPERBIRD

© WARNER BROS.-SEVEN ARTS. INC.

Introduction

Performance, Mopar Style

Chrysler Corporation's modern performance roots can be traced back to the 1951 introduction of the innovative Firepower V-8, a powerful design that debuted in the DeSoto ranks in 1952, and then as a Dodge offering the following year. Featuring an efficient cylinder head using hemispherical combustion chambers, the Firepower "Hemi" represented an impressive entry in Detroit's burgeoning horsepower race even if the cars it powered weren't particularly intimidating.

Chrysler rectified that situation by rolling out its famed 300 "letter-series" luxury performance models in 1955. Taking its name from the 300hp 331ci Hemi beneath its hood, the 1955 C-300 was the "most powerful sedan in the world," according to *Mechanix Illustrated*'s Tom McCahill. In 1956, all Chrysler divisions made moves into the fast lane as DeSoto's Adventurer, Dodge's D500, and Plymouth's Fury appeared, each capable of running with Detroit's best.

By 1959, Chrysler had discontinued the Hemi in favor of lighter, less-complicated wedge-head V-8s. In 1960, the wedge-heads could be ordered with the exotic "ram-induction" setup—two four-barrel carburetors mounted outboard of each valve cover on long individual-runner manifolds. A variation on the ram-induction theme helped put

Opposite page
Plymouth's Superbird, basically a NASCAR racer unleashed on the street, was indicative of both how far Chrysler Corporation officials would go to stay on top of the performance heap and the degree of competitiveness reached by the muscle car crowd in the late sixties. With a 426 Hemi behind its aerodynamic snout and its distinctive "towel rack" rear spoiler, the Superbird was a certified 200mph screamer on the superspeedways. Hot on the heels of Dodge's winged Charger Daytona of 1969, the 1970 Superbird flew down the superspeedways for one year before racing's rulemakers shot it down.

Dodge and Plymouth atop the factory super-stock field in 1962. Featuring a compact cross-ram intake, the 413 "Max Wedge" was a direct response to Pontiac's 421 Super Duty and Chevrolet's 409. In 1963, an enlarged 426 Max Wedge appeared, followed by the Hemi's return in awesome 426ci race-only form in 1964.

Once the ball was rolling, there was no stopping Mopar performance; seemingly countless hot models began appearing in all model lines. Plymouth debuted their Barracuda in April 1964, beating Ford's Mustang to market by two weeks, and offering Mopar fans a pony car alternative to Dearborn's sales phenomenon. Enhancing the early Barracuda's performance image was 1965's Formula S version, a sporty handler equipped with a 235hp 273ci small-block V-8. At the same time, Dodge's compact Dart was developing as a potential performer, receiving the 383ci big-block in 1968, followed by an outrageous 440ci-equipped GTS model in 1969.

After NASCAR officials banned the 426ci race Hemi following the 1964 season, Chrysler engineers returned to the drawing board and penned the legendary 426ci street Hemi. Beginning in 1966, the Hemi was offered optionally for Dodge and Plymouth mid-sized models. That same year the stunning Charger first appeared in intermediate ranks. Joining the Charger in Dodge's 1967 performance stable was the hot-blooded, 440ci big-block-equipped Coronet R/T—a muscle-bound package mirrored by Plymouth's 1967 GTX. Big news in 1968 came in the form of Plymouth's Road Runner and Dodge's Super Bee, each created as budget-minded supercars offering loads of performance with few frills.

In 1969, Dodge designers built two specially equipped models to homologate wind-cheating bodies for NASCAR competition. While the Charger 500 featured only a flush-mounted grille and rear window, the Charger Daytona represented a radical departure with its huge rear wing and lengthened snout. Plymouth applied similar tactics to the Road Runner in 1970, resulting in the Superbird.

Also new for 1969 was a 440 fed by three Holley two-barrel carburetors, known as the 440 Six Pack in Dodge trim, and the 440 Six Barrel when under Plymouth hoods. Special versions of the Road Runner and Super Bee models were built to showcase the tri-carb 440.

When the restyled E-body 'Cuda and Challenger appeared in 1970, either could be ordered with the triple-carb big-block or the dominating Hemi. The 440 option carried over into 1971, the last year before tightening emissions restrictions led to radical cutbacks. Although a few "unofficial" triple-carb 440s managed to slip into public hands in 1972, the 440 Six Pack, 440+6, and 426 Hemi were cancelled, signaling the end of Chrysler Corporation's glory days.

From 1966 to 1971, more than 11,000 426ci Hemi V-8s made their way into various Dodge and Plymouth intermediates and pony cars, with a few race-minded A-body Darts and Barracudas thrown in for good measure. Packing 425 real horses, the Hemi could transform almost any Mopar model into a 13sec boulevard bully. Ford fans can brag about their Cobra Jets, Chevy followers will forever worship the LS6 454, but for six years there was basically only one king of Main Street USA—the 426 Hemi.

Chapter 1

Going Fast in a Big Way

Letter Cars, Adventurers, and Golden Commandos

The logic behind the name was simple; the big car's 331ci Hemi V-8 produced 300hp—remarkable output for 1955—thus Chrysler's impressive luxury/performance sedan was named "300." Actually, the 1955 model was officially labelled "C-300" in honor of various Chrysler prototypes identified by monikers using the "C" prefix. Each succeeding model took on a letter of the alphabet, resulting in Chrysler's 300s being referred to as "letter cars."

Nomenclature aside, all 300s were incredible machines combining full-sized luxury with loads of power and healthy suspension componentry. Leather interiors were standard, and so was state-of-the-art performance. Even at 4,300lb, the C-300 could run 0–60mph in 9.6sec, only 0.5sec slower than the 1955 V-8 Corvette. Sales brochures called the C-300 "America's greatest performing motor car . . . with the speed of the wind, the maneuverability of a polo pony, the power to pass on the road safely." In 1956, the 300B became the first American car to surpass the magical one-horsepower-per-cubic-inch barrier, its optional 354ci Hemi V-8 pumping out an advertised 355hp.

Chrysler made an ill-advised attempt to offer fuel injection under the 300's hood in 1958, then dropped the big, heavy Hemi V-8

Opposite page
Although many questioned the 1961 Dodge Polara's looks, it's awfully tough to knock a glaring red convertible. Dodge's 1961 Polara was based on a 122in wheelbase—four inches longer than the lower-priced Dart—and was set apart from its lower echelon running mates by a revised tail with rocket-inspired taillights. Notice the small "500" badge to the right of the left taillight—the only outward clue of a 1961 D500's presence, though in 1961 chrome rockers and wheel opening trim were part of the package as well. D500s were also equipped with larger 8.20x15in tires.

Chrysler introduced a convertible 300 letter car in 1957, a model suited nicely to the totally new long, low, and wide body inspired by stylist Virgil Exner. While the previous two 300s in 1955 and 1956 borrowed their grilles from the prestigious Imperial, the restyled 1957 300 used a grille all its own. A functional scoop below each pair of headlights aided in brake cooling. Also new was improved ride and handling, courtesy of Chrysler's innovative torsion bar front suspension, and an enlarged 392ci Hemi V-8. According to *Motor Life*, the attractive 300C could run 0–60mph in 7.7sec.

in favor of the lighter wedge-head powerplant the following year. Ram induction became a standard feature in 1960, and the 413ci-powered 300G of 1961 was perhaps the strongest letter car offered. With 400hp and 495lb-ft of torque delivered at an incredibly low 2800rpm, the 300G was not for the timid. According to *Motor Trend*, "care needs to be exercised on accelerating turns from a dead stop to avoid trading ends, since the tremendous torque makes it very easy to get out of shape." After an eleven year reign as "America's most powerful production car," Chrysler's letter series ended with 1965's 300L.

Plymouth and DeSoto got in the luxury/performance act in 1956. Every bit as lavish as Chrysler's 300, DeSoto's Adventurer came on the scene with an exclusive dose of golden imagery, plush appointments, and awesome power courtesy of a 320hp 341ci Hemi V-8. A 1956 Adventurer ran 137mph on the sands of Daytona Beach and later turned a 144mph lap around the Chrysler proving ground track in Chelsea, Michigan. DeSoto continued to offer its high-powered, limited-edition performance sedan in hardtop and convertible form through 1959, after which the Adventurer nameplate became the commonplace label for the division's top models.

Plymouth tried a similar approach in 1956, introducing its own limited-edition performance model. Available in eggshell white only, the Fury carried its own share of golden imagery and was capable of kicking up some sand as well. Powered by a unique

Chrysler rolled out 484 300C convertibles (five for export) in 1957, a figure second only to the droptop 300K's total in 1964. Production of 300C hardtops totalled 1,737, with another thirty-one built for export. Full "300C" identification appeared on the lower rear quarters, while small "300" badges were found on the deck lid and in the grille.

240hp 303ci V-8, a Fury dashed down Daytona Beach at 124mph during speed tests in February 1956. Offered for three model runs in basically unchanged fashion, the Fury suffered the same fate as DeSoto's Adventurer, trading in its exclusive performance package for a role as Plymouth's flagship line in 1959.

Dodge's power brokers chose a different path. Instead of a high-profile, limited-edition muscle machine, they offered an optional performance package available for any model in the Dodge line from the Custom Royal

Chrysler's impressive 392ci Hemi V-8 was offered in two forms under the 300C's long hood: the 375hp standard with 9.25:1 compression and a 390hp version for $500 more. Included in the latter's power pack was a high-lift cam and increased compression (10:1). Behind either 392 Hemi was a three-speed manual or Torqueflite automatic transmission. The accordion-like unit at top center is the optional power brake booster.

Right
Following Chrysler's first letter car, the C-300, each succeeding 300 was identified in alphabetic progression, beginning with the 300B in 1956, the 300C in 1957, and so on. After the 300H came and went in 1962, Chrysler officials skipped over the letter "I" to avoid confusion with the Roman numeral "I." The last letter car, the 300L, appeared in 1965.

Lancer hardtop down to the Coronet sedan. Aimed at making Dodge a force in NASCAR competition, the 1956 D500 package included various heavy-duty components and a choice of two 315ci Hemi V-8s, one with 9.25:1 compression and a single Carter four-barrel rated at 260hp, another with two Carter four-barrels pumping out 295 horses. All that muscle translated into record-shattering D500 performances at Bonneville in 1956, as well as a third-place finish for Dodge in NASCAR Grand National competition that year. Although Dodge quickly fell from NASCAR's ranks, the D500 package carried on, still available on all models through 1961.

By the time the smaller, lighter Max Wedge Mopars hit the scene in 1962, full-sized performance from Dodge and Plymouth had all but faded away, leaving only Chrysler's 300 letter cars to carry on the legacy for three more years.

Because Dodge's hot D500 was an optional performance package, it could be found in any guise from mundane four-door sedan to sexy convertible. The D500 equipment was introduced in 1956 and offered in various forms until 1961. Estimates put total production for the six-year model run at a mere 3,000. Consequently, D500 convertibles, like this 1957 Coronet, are exceptionally rare. Unlike the initial 1956 rendition, which featured various heavy-duty chassis components such as big Chrysler brakes, the 1957 D500 used standard Dodge running gear.

Left
As with all D500-equipped Dodges, the only outward identification on this 1957 D500 Coronet convertible is the small "500" badge on the deck lid. *Motor Trend* tested a 1957 Coronet four-door sedan with the 285hp D500 package and recorded a 0–60mph run of 9.4sec and quarter-mile performance of 17.2sec at 79mph. *Sports Car Illustrated* hotfoots did *Motor Trend* one better at the wheel of a 1957 D500 two-door Coronet hardtop, running 0–60mph in 8.5sec with a 16.6 quarter-mile time. Terminal speed was 83mph. The attractive wire wheels on this rarely seen D500 convertible were dealer-installed options in 1957.

Chrysler Corporation began the muscle car era when it introduced its first V–8. The hemispherical head engine unleashed a performance war. . . .

—Randy Leffingwell,
American Muscle

Again, two levels of D500 performance were available in 1957. This 285hp 325ci D500 V-8 featured solid lifters, 10:1 compression, and a single Carter four-barrel carburetor. Top of the heap was the Super D500, a 310hp version of the 325ci Hemi fed by twin Carter four-barrels. Price for the basic D500 powertrain option was $113.65. *Sports Car Illustrated* called the 285hp D500 V-8 "a well-balanced engine—not so big that it won't rev, and not so small that it lacks torque. As a result it delivers plenty of usable horsepower all the way up the line."

Offered in nearly identical, exclusive fashion from 1956 to 1958, Plymouth's Fury featured one shade only—Buckskin Beige (1956 models were eggshell white), a color not available on any other model. A complete array of golden imagery inside and out complemented this soft shade. At $3,032, this 1958 Fury was the only Plymouth that year priced above $3,000. Production in 1958 was 5,303, following totals of 7,438 in 1957 and 4,485 in 1956.

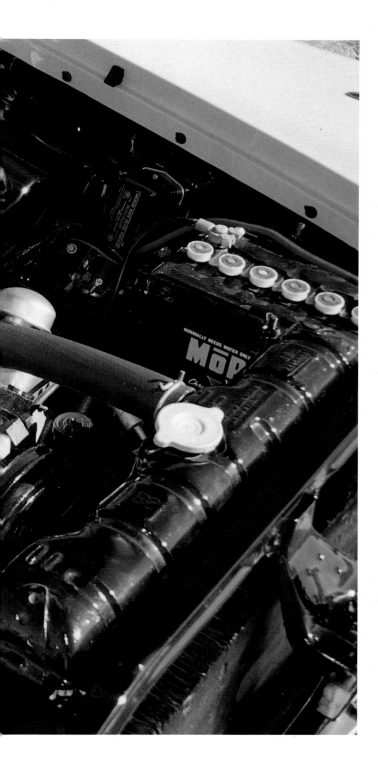

DeSoto offered its last limited-edition Adventurer luxury/performance cruiser in 1959. Standard features included power steering, power brakes, a padded dash, and a distinctive brushed aluminum sidesweep done in gold. In typical fashion, gold dress-up was also found in the grille and on the wheel covers. Inside, swivel bucket seats were introduced in 1959 as another standard Adventurer feature. Beneath the hood was a 350hp 383ci V-8 topped with two Carter four-barrel carburetors. Only 590 Adventurer hardtops were built in 1959, accompanied by a mere ninety-seven convertibles.

Left
Standard power for the 1957 and 1958 Fury was the "Dual Fury V-800" (shown here), a high-performance 318ci powerplant not available under other Plymouth hoods. Twin Carter four-barrels, 9.25:1 compression, a high-lift cam, a dual-point distributor, and dual exhausts all added up to 295hp. In 1958, the Dual Fury V-800 was joined by the optional Golden Commando 350ci V-8 rated at 305hp. The 1958 Golden Commando V-8 option was priced at $324 and offered on all Plymouth models.

Previous pages
Plymouth diluted the Fury image considerably in 1959, transferring the once-proud nameplate to its topline models, which meant a four-door Fury would hit the streets for the first time. Preserving some of the previous limited-edition image was the new Sport Fury, offered in two-door hardtop and convertible form. Sport Fury buyers were also presented with a wide array of color choices. Power came from a "Fury V-800" powerplant with "Super Pak"—a 260hp 318ci V-8 featuring a high-lift cam, 9:1 compression, free-flowing dual exhausts, and a Carter AFB four-barrel carburetor. Another reminder of the early Fury was the optional Golden Commando 395 V-8, an engine named for the 395lb-ft of torque it delivered.

Plymouth's Golden Commando V-8 was a $74 option displacing 361ci and making 305hp with the aid of 10:1 compression, a high-lift cam, special low-restriction dual exhausts, and a Carter four-barrel. Gold dress-up on the air cleaner and valve covers helped preserve the Fury tradition.

Right
Dodge's D500 option was available in a variety of forms in 1960 and 1961 and could be fitted to either the topline Polaras or the shorter, less prestigious Darts. In 1961, the "Dart D500" powerplant was a 305hp 361ci V-8, while the Polara version was based on the larger 383ci engine, both with single four-barrel carburetors. The wire wheels are a dealer-installed option.

In 1960, all D500 Dodges, Polara or Dart, featured the intriguing ram-induction setup with its long, spider-like manifolds. Offered for the last time in 1961, the D500 option was still available in ram induction form, but the basic package relied on a single Carter four-barrel carburetor on a conventional intake, as shown here. The "Polara D500" V-8 was a 383ci powerplant rated at 325hp with 10:1 compression. Polara D500s mated to the Torqueflite automatic came standard with 3.23:1 rear gears. Reportedly, a 1961 Polara D500 could hit 60mph from rest in 8.9sec.

No one did gadgetry better than the Chrysler Corporation. This fully loaded 1961 Polara convertible features a speedometer that allowed natural light to shine through for illumination, a rectangular steering wheel (for increased leg room), and the optional "Hi-Way Hi-Fi," a record player mounted beneath the dash above the transmission tunnel.

Left

The 1964 300K is considered by many to be the last great Chrysler 300 as its successor, the 1965 300L, was toned down considerably in the performance department. The 300K was the last letter car offered with the exotic ram-induction option, which looked every bit as impressive as it performed. Production of 300K hardtops reached 3,022, the highest total in the eleven-year letter-car history. Convertible production in 1964 was 625.

Standard power for the 1964 300K came from a 360hp 413ci big-block V-8 fed by a single four-barrel. Available at extra cost was a 390hp 413 topped by twin Carter AFB four-barrels on spider-like ram-induction aluminum intake manifolds. Introduced as a standard 300 feature in 1960, ram induction made its final appearance under the 300K's hood. Compression for the 390hp ram-induction 413, at 9.6:1, was actually lower than the 360hp, single-four-barrel version, which squeezed fuel and air at a 10:1 ratio.

Chapter 2

The A Team

Darts, Demons, & Dusters

A Dodge named Dart first appeared as a radically aerodynamic showcar in 1956. Four years later, the Dart returned as a new downsized regular production model rolling on a 118in wheelbase, four inches shorter than Dodge's Polara flagship. Also new for 1960 was unitized body construction and an impressive powertrain option called ram-induction. A "poorman's supercharger" of sorts, ram-induction helped make Dodges and Plymouths formidable forces at the dragstrip, establishing a legacy that grew in prominence with each passing year.

Another downsizing maneuver and further development of the ram-induction design in 1962 raised the racing stakes even higher. A smaller, lighter Dart based on a 116in wheelbase established the platform parameters, while the outrageous 413ci Max Wedge supplied the power. Crowned with a considerably more compact cross-ram intake, the Max Wedge V-8 transformed Dodges and Plymouths into intimidating 13sec super-stocks right off the truck. A 1962 Plymouth Max Wedge eventually became the first "production car" to break the 12sec quarter mile barrier. A second-edition 1963 Max Wedge displacing 426ci left the competition even further behind.

That same year, Dodge transferred the Dart banner to a new compact model leading up to the development of Chrysler's A-body family. Initially offered only with six-cylinder

Opposite page
Perhaps the most nimble of Dodge's high-profile 1969 "Scat Pack," which included the R/T versions of the Charger and Coronet, the Dart GTS could be quickly identified by its standard twin hood bulges, various emblems, and twin exhaust trumpets. Popular "bumblebee" stripes for the tail were available at extra cost. Changes for 1969 included transferring the formerly standard GTS Dart's bucket seats to the options list.

Dodge's new 1960 Dart was smaller and less expensive than the topline Polara and possessed some serious performance potential when equipped with the D500 option. First made available in 1956, Dodge's D500 performance package was offered for Polaras and the three Dart models, Seneca, Pioneer, and Phoenix. Most prominent among D500 equipment in 1960 was the new ram-induction setup featuring twin four-barrels on long, individual-runner aluminum intake manifolds. In Polara ranks, the D500 option was available for the 383ci V-8, while Darts used a smaller 361ci version, though apparently it was possible to order the Polara's big 383ci D500 V-8 in the smaller Dart. *Sports Car Illustrated* wrote that a ram-inducted 1960 Dart "can make other road users a trifle sheepish at stop light showdowns."

power, the Dart GT first flexed a little muscle in 1964 when the 273ci small-block V-8 was made an option. Things really got hot four years later when the 275hp 340ci V-8 was introduced. The 340 was standard equipment for the 1968 Dart GTS and transformed Dodge's A-body into a serious quarter-mile threat, a fact *Car Life* verified with a 14.68sec ET topping out at 96.2 mph. And if that wasn't enough, the optional 383ci big-block promised even more. At the top of 1968's A-body heap was the awesome Hurst built, Hemi-powered Dart, an all-out racing counterpart to Plymouth's Hemi Barracudas.

In 1969, Dodge offered a 440-powered Dart GTS, a boulevard brute inspired by transplants performed by Chicago's legendary Mopar performance mogul Norm Krause, alias "Mr. Norm," of Grand-Spaulding Dodge. Roughly 600 440 GTS Darts were built in 1969, again with the help of the Hurst crew.

Contrasting with the big-block A-bodies was the new Dart Swinger 340, the smallest and most affordable member of Dodge's 1969 Scat Pack. Ads described the 275hp Swinger 340 as "6000 rpm for less than $3,000." *Car Life*'s staff was so impressed with the Swinger 340's performance (14.8sec at 96mph in the quarter-mile) that they named it their "Best Compact" for 1969.

Inspired by Plymouth's success with the A-body Duster 340, a performance car for the budget-minded, Dodge designers traded the Swinger 340 for the Demon 340 in 1971. Plymouth's Duster 340 was introduced in 1970 and based on a Valiant platform with a

"fastback" of sorts grafted on. When equipped with the yeoman 340 small-block, both the Duster and Demon were capable of low-14sec blasts down the quarter-mile, putting them among Detroit's best bangs for the buck as the seventies dawned.

With performance de-escalation coming after 1971, Mopar's A-team was eventually disbanded; Dodge's Demon was gone by 1973, which was the last year for the 340. Armed with the optional 360ci small-block, Plymouth's Duster carried on in 1974, along with a Dart Sport counterpart from Dodge, but it just wasn't the same.

Since the D500's long ram-induction manifolds created a supercharging effect, this hot 361ci V-8 didn't require a major dose of high compression to up the power ante. At 10:1, the 1960 361ci Dart D500 V-8's compression level was typical for the day. Output was 310hp and 435lb-ft of torque, which translated into 0–60mph in the 8sec range. Mid-range power, however, was the D500's forte. As *Motor Trend*'s Walt Woron wrote, "the response when both carburetors cut in is instantaneous. It comes on with a roar, pushing you back in your seat, and the car leaps ahead like a ram rushing to butt a challenger."

Left
The small, vertical "500" badge on the deck lid of this 1960 Dart Phoenix was the only giveaway to this Dodge's status as a dominating D500 street warrior. Offered for the last time in 1961, the D500 option was toned down with a standard four-barrel offering in addition to the now optional ram-induction version (in 1960, all D500s were ram-induction cars). Reportedly only about 3,000 D500s were built between 1956 and 1961.

Two versions of the 413 Max Wedge were offered to Plymouth and Dodge buyers in 1962, the difference in output determined by the compression ratio chosen. The 410hp version featured 11:1 compression, while the 420hp 413 squeezed the mixture to the tune of 13.5:1. "Max" referred to the Maximum Performance label used in factory brochures, "Wedge" described the 413's wedge-shaped combustion chambers (as opposed to Dodge's earlier Hemispherical design). In Dodge ranks, the 413 Max Wedge was offered in all models from the bare-bones Dart 330 to the trimmed-out Polara 500. Since most racers preferred the lighter, cheaper Darts, Max Wedge Polaras like this one are exceptionally rare. Total production for all 1962 Max Wedges, Dodge and Plymouth, was about 300.

Previous pages
Priced at $374.40, the 410hp 413 was as affordable as it was powerful, leading *Motor Trend*'s Roger Huntington to claim it offered "more performance per dollar than any other factory-assembled car in America." Huntington also liked the Max Wedge's free-flowing cast-iron headers, calling them "a work of art—far and away the most efficient ever put on an American car." Behind those headers was a dual exhaust system that featured cutouts that could be unbolted for unsilenced, wide-open running. During Huntington's road test, a 1962 Max Wedge Dodge managed 0–60mph in 5.8sec and produced a 14.4sec, 100mph quarter-mile ET. With the exhaust cutouts unbolted and optional 9in tires in back, the car eventually turned a sizzling 13.44sec, 109.76mph ET.

Manufactured under precise conditions at Chrysler's Marine and Industrial Division, the 413 Max Wedge V-8 was a no-nonsense racing powerplant not intended for everyday operation. Heavy-duty dual valve springs in the heads meant valve seals couldn't be installed, making the Max Wedge a serious oil burner, but lubricant consumption was of no concern to a drag racer. Everything else about the Max Wedge was bullet-proof from top to bottom. A reinforced block and heads, a forged steel crank, Magnafluxed forged steel connecting rods, lightweight aluminum pistons, beefed-up valvetrain, and a deep-sump oil pan added up to one formidable powerplant. Topping it off were two Carter AFB carbs mounted diagonally on a cross-ram intake featuring 15in individual runners.

With the Dart nameplate moved down to Dodge's compact ranks, most 1963 Max Wedges appeared as stripped-down, inexpensive 330 models, with a few upscale Polaras again thrown in for good measure. New for 1963 was an optional, weight-saving aluminum front end with a distinctive scooped hood. The light front end helped trim the car's weight to 3200 pounds, which in turn made the 1963 426 Max Wedge Dodge an easy 12sec performer. As 1963 advertisements claimed, "when a Dodge loses these days, it's to another Dodge."

No extra baggage here; this 1963 Dodge 330 was meant for racing, not impressing the neighbors. Notice the dash-mounted push button transmission controls directly to the left of the steering wheel. Chrysler Corporation's excellent three-speed Torqueflite was Detroit's first automatic transmission capable of standing up to serious torque loads. From the beginning, automatic-backed Max Wedge Mopars were kings of drag racing's Stock/Automatic classes.

Left
Under Dodge hoods, the 413 or 426 Max Wedge was known as a "Ramcharger" V-8; Plymouth used the "Super Stock" moniker. As in 1962, the 426 Ramcharger V-8 for 1963 was offered in two forms, one with 11:1 compression and 415hp, the other with a head-cracking 13.5:1 squeeze and 425 horses. The two foam rubber "doughnuts" atop the carburetors sealed to the aluminum hood's underside allowing the functional scoop to supply cooler, denser air directly into the twin Carter AFBs.

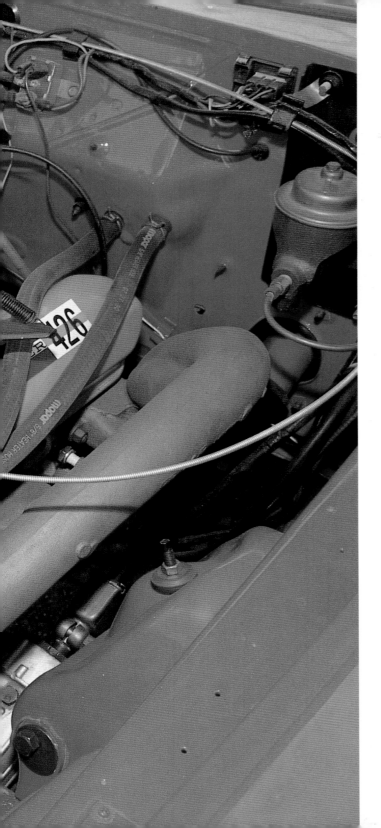

Left
Dodge had offered a GT package for its compact Dart since the car's introduction in 1963, but early Dart GTs offered more sporty flair than actual performance. Then along came the 1968 Dart GTS, or GTSport. With a 275hp 340 as standard equipment, the Dart GTS was more than capable of holding its own. And for only $25 more, the 340 could've been traded for a 383ci big-block. This 1969 GTS 340 hardtop is one of 3,919 built.

Simulated vents in the twin hood bulges announced the GTS Dart's underhood contents, in this case the standard 275hp 340ci small-block, a popular powerplant that appeared throughout the Mopar muscle car ranks from 1968 to 1973. A collection of heavy-duty suspension equipment complemented the affordable, easy-to-handle 340 as part of the GTS performance package.

Left

Dodge introduced the Demon a year after Plymouth's Duster debuted in 1970. In the best GTS tradition, the Demon 340 was everything its A-body forerunners were and more. Along with the 275hp small-block, the Demon 340 came standard with a heavy-duty three-speed manual, Rallye suspension consisting of beefed-up torsion bars and a stiffer sway bar up front, heavier leaves in back, and upgraded shocks all around. A long list of options could both dress up the Demon 340 and punch up the power. But even in base form a Demon could turn the quarter in about 14.5sec. The tires, widened rear rims, and locking gas cap on this Panther Pink 1971 Demon 340 are owner-installed modifications.

From its 1968 inception, Mopar's 340ci small-block was a performance-minded powerplant that offered punch without the weight disadvantage typical to the 383ci big-block. Advertised output was 275hp at 5000rpm and 340lb-ft of torque at 3200rpm. Compression was 10.3:1. Production of Demon 340s in 1971 reached 10,098.

W e decided to make it a sleeper that would blow the doors off hulking, pretentious behemouths twice its size.

—1970 Plymouth brochure

Probably most commonly seen in E-body Barracudas and Challengers in 1971, this dictation recorder with its remote microphone wasn't exactly the type of performance equipment you'd expect to find in a 340-powered Dodge Demon.

Right
Plymouth rejoined Mopar's A-body performance ranks in 1970 with the Duster 340, a hot model that quickly qualified as a candidate for the Rapid Transit System, Plymouth's version of Dodge's Scat Pack. As advertisements explained, the Rapid Transit System wouldn't accept "any car that can't cut a 14-second quarter." According to *Car and Driver*, a 1970 Duster 340 put up a 14.39sec, 97.2mph ET—case closed. Production of 1972 Duster 340s, like this fully loaded Plum Crazy model, was 15,681.

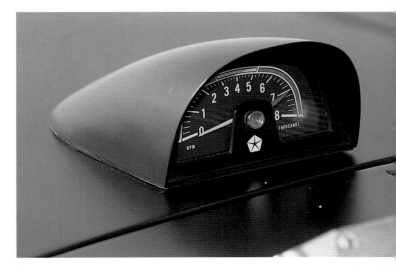

This 8000rpm hood tach was among the many options available to Duster 340 buyers. Although both Demons and Dusters were affordable performance machines in base form, they got expensive in a hurry once buyers started checking-off boxes on the order sheet. A twin-scooped hood, rear spoiler, and Rallye wheels were among the most popular A-body add-ons.

Left
With real performance on the wane by 1971, splashy graphics and assorted imagery pieces became more popular. This blacked-out hood with "340 Wedge" identification was one of many available A-body dress-up items. Even in net-rated 240hp form, the Duster 340's small-block was still a hot little number in 1972.

Chapter 3

'Cudas & Challengers

Chrysler Corporation's Pony Cars

Even though Plymouth actually beat Ford to market by two weeks with its Barracuda, it was Dearborn's wildly popular Mustang that helped inspire the "pony car" label for the new long-hood/short-deck automotive breed. Introduced in April 1964, Plymouth's first pony car was basically a Valiant with a large glass "fastback" tacked on, an image that nonetheless came off remarkably fresh. Performance, however, was timid, at least until the Formula S version appeared in 1965. The S sported a 235hp 273ci Commando V-8, heavy-duty suspension, and four Goodyear Blue Streaks on wide 14in wheels.

A totally restyled Barracuda based on a larger A-body platform emerged in 1967, making room for Dodge's 383ci big-block V-8, a 280hp option for the Formula S and standard Barracudas. The following year, the Formula S model's base 273ci V-8 was exchanged for the hot little 275hp 340ci small-block, a derivative of the 273. According to *Car Life*, a 1968 340 Barracuda could trip the lights at the far end of the quarter-mile in 14.97sec.

Hottest of the A-body Barracudas were the 1968 Super Stock models. Armed with 425 Hemi horses, Super Stocks were capable of 10sec blasts down the quarter right out of the box. At least fifty of these race-ready Hemi Barracudas were built by Hurst in

Opposite page
Although it retained the previous A-body Barracuda's 108in wheelbase, just about everything else on Plymouth's new E-body platform represented a radical departure from past Mopar pony car practices. To emphasize the E-body's sporty image, Chrysler introduced a wild array of radiant paint schemes with equally wild names, including such shades as Go-Mango, Sublime, In Violet, and Plum Crazy. This Hemi-powered 1970 'Cuda hardtop is one of 284 built with a four-speed—another 368 were equipped with Torqueflites.

Under the direction of the Chrysler Advanced Styling Studio's Cliff Voss, designers began work in 1967 on the totally new, third-generation Barracuda. The bulk of the credit for Plymouth's exciting 1970 pony car goes to stylist John Herlitz. Three models were offered, the Barracuda and the upscale Gran Coupe, both powered by six-cylinders in base-form, and the 'Cuda, which featured a 335hp 383ci big-block as standard equipment. Optional 'Cuda performance powerplants included the 275hp 340ci small-block, the 375hp 440ci four-barrel, the 390hp 440+6 (with three Holley two-barrels) and the 425hp 426ci Hemi.

Detroit. Better suited for the street, yet still not meant for the meek, the 1969 'Cuda 440 featured 375hp and 480lb-ft of torque. A bit tough to live with as an everyday driver as power steering and power front discs couldn't be included due to space restrictions, the 440 'Cuda was nonetheless a certified 13sec street killer.

Mopar's pony car line-up received a totally new E-body shell in 1970 as Plymouth's Barracuda was joined by Dodge's Challenger, a small sporty package that resembled its corporate cousin but was two inches longer. Honoring the long-hood/short-deck theme to even greater extremes than their predecessors, the revitalized Barracuda and newborn Challenger turned heads with ease.

The huge Shaker hood scoop, standard on Hemi 'Cudas, was functional, but also assisted greatly in the image department. With the Shaker removed, the 426 Hemi's twin Carter AFB (aluminum four-barrel) carburetors are revealed. Hemi 'Cuda performance was simply awesome—according to *Car Craft*, the quarter-mile flew by in 13.10sec. Trap speed was 107.1mph.

High-back buckets, the distinctive "Tuff" steering wheel, and the trademark Pistol Grip four-speed shifter added a sporty touch to the 1970 Hemi 'Cuda's interior. Also visible are a 150mph speedometer and 8000rpm tach.

As for beauty beneath the skin, both Mopar E-bodies were available with an incredible variety of performance options, beginning with the potent 340 small-block, escalating up to the 383 big-block, going overboard with a 440+6 or 440 Six Pack, and peaking with the awesome 426 Hemi. At one end of the scale, 340 'Cudas and Challengers were quick, nimble road cars; at the other end, the nose-heavy 440 and Hemi cars were boulevard brutes with one thing in mind: travelling a straight line from point A to point B as rapidly as possible. During the muscle car's heyday from 1970 to 1971, they didn't come much quicker than a Hemi-powered E-body Mopar.

The Hemi fell by the wayside after 1971, but 'Cudas and Challengers carried on in relatively sporty fashion, with the still-warm 340 small-block representing the hottest underhood option. Like the brutish big-block V-8s, convertible E-bodies were discontinued after 1971, and the Barracuda/Challenger line itself appeared for the last time in 1974.

Created to homologate a road racing relative for SCCA Trans Am competition, Dodge's T/A Challenger hit the streets in March 1970. T/A Challengers were powered by a 340 Six Pack small-block V-8 unique to the application and equipped with a host of standard performance equipment including heavy-duty suspension, a Hurst-shifted four-speed, and racing-type cutout exhausts. Ads promised a second T/A Challenger rendition in 1971, but the idea was cancelled in 1970. Only 2,399 T/As were built. Another 2,724 nearly identical AAR (a reference to Dan Gurney's "All American Racing" team which built and raced the Trans Am version) 'Cuda models were produced for 1970.

Dodge's T/A Challenger and Plymouth's AAR 'Cuda were probably the first Detroit performance machines with mismatched rubber—G60 Goodyear tires in back, E60s in front (this car has non-stock aftermarket treads). Although most T/A Challengers wear the optional Rallye wheels, the standard rims were these 15x7JJ steel units with center caps and trim rings. Also standard were cutout exhausts, which helped in the image department but did little for performance since the exhaust plumbing required to make the system work, was overly restrictive. Many owners dumped this arrangement in favor of a conventional rear-exiting system.

Left
Built from the oil pan up as a serious performance power-source, the 340 Six Pack featured a recast block with a reinforced lower end, reworked cylinder heads with ample room for porting, a beefed-up valvetrain, and 10.5:1 compression. Three Holley two-barrels on an aluminum Edelbrock intake fed the beast. Output was conservatively listed at 290hp, 15hp more than the equally underrated standard 340 four-barrel V-8. Actual Trans Am racing Challengers were powered by a destroked 305ci version of the 340 and produced an amazing 440hp.

A large rubber gasket around the 340 Six Pack V-8's air cleaner sealed the unit to the underside of this fiberglass hood, allowing cooler denser air to flow through its racing-style snorkel scoop directly to the three Holleys. Engineers discovered that elevating the scoop's snout about one inch above the hood helped circumvent the induction-inhibiting boundary layer of slow-moving air that normally develops at speed, a trick that was reportedly worth another 10 or 15hp at 80mph.

Right
Helping set the hotter 1970 'Cuda models apart from their sedate Barracuda and Gran Coupe brethren were standard fog lights below the bumper and a sport hood with twin scoops. The eye-catching Shaker hood, a standard feature on Hemi 'Cudas, was optional with all other V-8s. 'Cudas also included various heavy-duty suspension pieces. In back, beefy leaf springs featured five full leaves with two half leaves on the left, and six full leaves on the right. Stiffer shocks all around and thicker 0.92in torsion bars up front working in concert with an enlarged 0.94in stabilizer bar helped keep all that torque under control. The popular Rallye wheels were optional. This 1970 440+6 'Cuda hardtop, one of 1,755 built, features the Shaker hood as well as the "hockey stick" engine identification stripes on the rear quarter

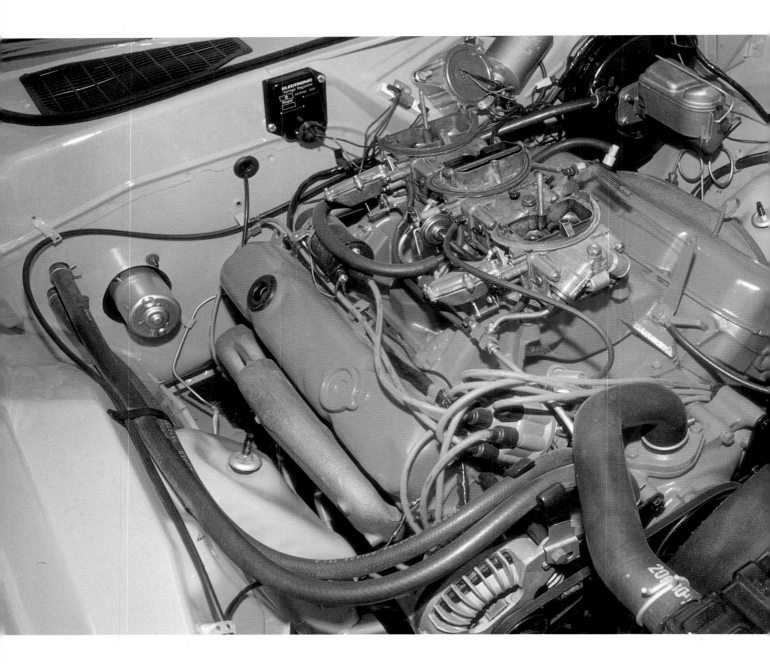

Hiding beneath this 1970 'Cuda's Shaker scoop are three Holley two-barrels atop the impressive 390hp 440 big-block. Under Plymouth pony car hoods, this setup was known as the 440+6; identical Dodge versions wore the 440 Six Pack label. Internal features of the 440+6 included a forged-steel crank, heavy-duty connecting rods, and reinforced, cast-aluminum 10.5:1 pistons.

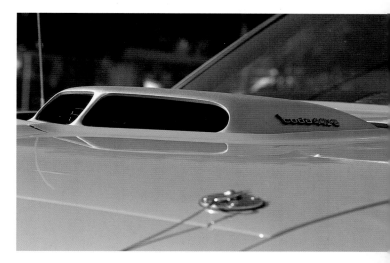

The unforgettable Shaker scoop did just that—lurching and shaking considerably when a 440+6 'Cuda's pedal went to the metal. Offered in Argent Silver, matte black or body color, Shakers were standard atop 426 Hemis and optional on all other 1970–71 'Cuda and Challenger V-8s.

Following pages
With its 110-inch wheelbase stretched two inches longer than its E-body counterpart from Plymouth, Dodge's Challenger differed just enough to not be accused of being a rubber-stamp mirror image. Sheet metal differences between the Challenger and 'Cuda were considerable. The Challenger's most unique exterior features are its beltline crease and quad headlights. Convertible E-bodies were built for 1970 and 1971 only; this Plum Crazy 1971 Challenger droptop is one of 2,165 built.

I t snarls, it quivers,
it leaps vast prairies at a
single bound.
    —1970 Challenger brochure

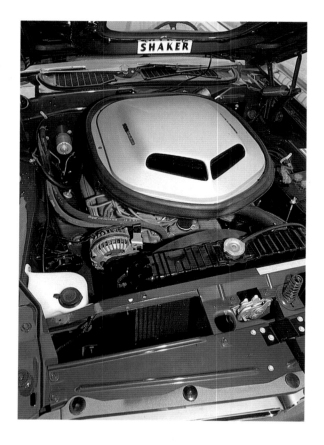

Standard power source for the Challenger R/T ("Road and Track"), the 383 Magnum V-8 was optional for all other Challengers. Mandated decompression dropped the 383 Magnum's output from 335hp in 1970 to 300hp in 1971, but the aging big-block was still one tough customer under an E-body's hood. Reportedly, only 126 1971 Challenger convertibles were built with the 383 Magnum backed by the Torqueflite automatic.

When fully equipped with all the optional goodies like buckets, console with floor shift, and a sport steering wheel, Challengers were as sporty inside as they were out. The orange knob below the dash at the head of the console controlled the Shaker hood scoop's cool air induction system.

Chapter 4

Big, Bad B-Bodies

Mopar's Mid-Sized Muscle

Chrysler Corporation's all-out 1964 426ci race Hemi enjoyed only one race season before NASCAR moguls killed it with a change to the minimum production homologation requirements. Chrysler's initial response was to pull out of NASCAR racing for the 1965 season, but the Mopar crew returned in 1966 following development of a new, "detuned" 426 Hemi. The new engine was built with everyday street operation in mind, if only to appease sanctioning bodies who liked to see so-called stock cars race in stock classes.

Although the 426ci street Hemi was indeed detuned in comparison to its racing forefather, it was by no means emasculated. *Motor Trend* noted that "you can buy Plymouth's intermediate-sized Belvedere, right off the showroom floor, with a '426 Hemi' and have a darn good chance of winning [your] class in A/ or AA/Stock [drag racing] right off the bat with only minor modifica-

tions." With 425hp on tap, the 426 Hemi immediately transformed all Mopar B-bodies into high-13sec screamers.

Most stylish among the early high-powered B-bodies was Dodge's Charger, which

Opposite page
Introduced mid-year in 1969, Dodge's Six Pack Super Bee was the epitome of no-frills performance. Wheel covers weren't even included in the package, nor were hood hinges—the fiberglass hood with its huge functional scoop simply lifted off once pins were released at all four corners. Beneath that hood was a 390hp 440 big-block topped by three Holley two-barrels. In exchange for an incredibly low $3,138 asking price, Six Pack Super Bee customers received a streetwise strip challenger capable of turning 13.8sec quarters. Dodge built 817 Six Pack Super Bee hardtops like this one in 1969 and another 615 coupe versions. Plymouth also offered a similar 440 Six Barrel Road Runner for 1969. The non-functional rear quarter scoops shown here were optional pieces.

The famed 426 street Hemi debuted in 1966 to rave reviews and was available in Dodge Chargers and Coronets and Plymouth Belvederes and upscale Satellites. Test drive results varied, with *Car and Driver's* 13.80sec quarter-mile dash in a 1966 Hemi Satellite ranking among the quickest. This gold 1966 Plymouth Belvedere II convertible is one of only six equipped with the 425hp 426 Hemi and Torqueflite automatic transmission that year. Four other 1966 Hemi Satellite convertibles were built with four-speeds.

was basically a mundane Coronet shell radically transformed through the addition of hideaway headlights and a sloping fastback roofline. Introduced along with the street Hemi in 1966, the Charger's interior featured four bucket seats and a console. Not nearly as radical but equally sporty, Plymouth's GTX appeared in 1967 showcasing a new pumped-up 375hp version of the 440ci big-block V-8 introduced the previous year, a power source that offered almost as much performance potential as the Hemi for a fraction of the cost.

In 1968, Plymouth and Dodge kicked off the "budget supercar" race, introducing the Road Runner and Super Bee, respectively. The base-model versions of these hot B-bodies were bare-bones bombers with frills spared in favor of pure performance. Standard equipment included a specially prepared 335hp 383ci big-block backed by a four-speed. Price was just short of $3,000, and quarter mile performance measured just this side of 100mph. Carrying the budget supercar idea one step further, Dodge and Plymouth introduced the Six Pack Super Bee and Six Barrel Road Runner for 1969, each a stripped-down, strip-ready racer with 390 horses beneath a lift-off fiberglass hood.

B-body aggression escalated to an even higher level in 1969 with the coming of Dodge's NASCAR-inspired aero fliers, the Charger 500 and Charger Daytona. Built to homologate wind-cheating variants for competition on NASCAR's superspeedways, the Charger 500 featured a blunt nose with a

flush-mounted grille and a similar treatment in back where the standard Charger's drag-intensive tunneled backlight was traded for flush-mounted glass. Although the tricks improved the B-body's high-speed character-istics, the Charger 500 still wasn't the answer to Ford's challenge on the NASCAR circuit, a

The radical 426 race Hemi had featured individual-tube headers and twin carbs mounted diagonally on a cross-ram intake, but 1966's slightly civilized street Hemi was equipped with a more conventional inline, dual four-barrel intake and cast-iron exhaust manifolds. Output was 425hp at 5500rpm and 480lb-ft of torque.

"Leader of the Dodge Rebellion" was how advertisements labeled the exciting 1966 Dodge Charger. Like Plymouth's little Barracuda, which was basically a Valiant with a huge rear window tacked on, Dodge's Charger was essentially a ho-hum Coronet under that sloping fastback and behind those hideaway headlights, a resemblance made more obvious when the lights were exposed. Nonetheless, the look came off remarkably well. Inside, the Charger was far from ho-hum with four buckets and a long console as standard sporty features. When armed with the optional 426 Hemi, all that sporty imagery was backed up by true performance with 0–60mph coming in about 7sec. Dodge built 468 Hemi Chargers for 1966 and a mere twenty-seven the following year.

The Charger's innovative interior featured two rear bucket seats that, along with the center armrest, folded to form a flat storage area accessible through the trunk. The view shown here is the passenger area of a 1967 Charger.

fact that lead to the development of the winged Daytona beginning in June 1969. With an aerodynamic snout and towering rear spoiler, the Charger Daytona was capable of 200mph on the high banks, as was Plymouth's 1970 Road Runner-based version, the Superbird. After shattering various NASCAR records, Mopar's winged warriors were banned following the 1970 season.

A totally restyled B-body emerged in 1971 as the Charger, Road Runner, and GTX made their last stand as truly muscular performers. Plymouth's GTX was discontinued after 1971, as were the tri-carb 440s and the vaunted Hemi. And once the relatively warm 340 small-block disappeared after 1973, Mopar's B-body performance tale officially came to a close.

Standard 1967 GTX features included "GTX" emblems on the fenders and deck lid, a racing-style pop-open gas cap, twin bright exhaust trumpets, and Red Streak rubber. Also standard was Chrysler's tough Torqueflite three-speed automatic, with a four-speed available at extra cost. Five-spoke Magnum 500 sport wheels and twin black stripes were also GTX options. "GTO owners had better look to their defenses," concluded *Car and Driver.*

Previous pages
Considered an "executive's hot rod," Plymouth's GTX made the scene in 1967 loaded with attractive equipment. A twin-scooped hood and an interior featuring somewhat plush appointments and a center console were certainly impressive, but the real news was the GTX's standard 375hp 440ci big-block V-8, subtly identified within the hood ornament. Heavy-duty suspension and beefy drum brakes were included as well, and if that wasn't enough, the optional 426 Hemi stood waiting in the wings. In all, Plymouth rolled out 11,970 440-equipped GTX hardtops and convertibles in 1967; another 108 hardtops and seventeen convertibles were built with the Hemi.

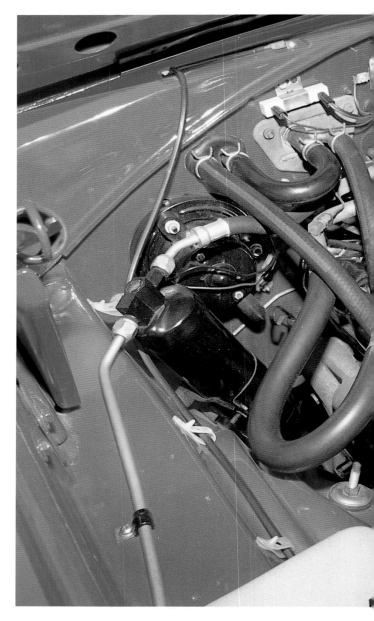

Used initially as a torque mill for Chrysler's luxury barges, the 440 was modified in 1967 and reintroduced as the Super Commando V-8, a 375hp big-block installed as standard equipment under the GTX's twin scoops. The Super

Commando package included revised valvetrain gear, free-flowing exhausts, and a windage tray in the oil pan. With 10.1:1 compression, the 375hp 440 produced 480lb-ft of torque at 3200rpm. According to *Car and Driver*, "The Plymouth boys have breathed new life into the old 440 engine to produce a new monster capable of blowing off everything including a street Hemi up to 100 mph."

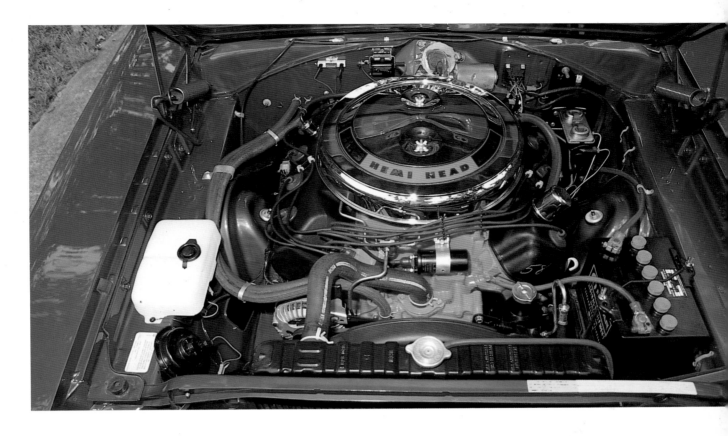

Left
Plymouth's 1968 Road Runner—designed for customers who preferred going fast but didn't like paying for a lot of irrelevant extras—inspired a rash of so-called "budget supercars" out of Detroit. Dress-up items were kept to a bare minimum, with design efforts instead concentrating on underhood contents. Standard power came from a modified 383ci big-block featuring the cam, heads, exhaust manifolds, and windage tray from the big brother 440. A four-speed was also standard. "The Road Runner is the simplest, most brazenly pure, non-compromising supercar in history," claimed *Motor Trend*. In a *Super Stock & Drag Illustrated* test, a 335hp 383 Road Runner put up a 14.27sec, 92mph ET.

Although Road Runners were relatively affordable performance packages in standard form, a long list of options promised to both raise the bottom line as well as straight-line potential. Most prominent on the list was the ever-present 425hp 426 Hemi, priced at roughly $715. Various mandatory options accompanied the Hemi, such as the $138.90 Sure-Grip Dana 60 rearend with 3.54:1 gears, and drove the final tally for a Hemi Road Runner well beyond the $2,986 base price. Production of 1968 Road Runner Hemi coupes was 840. Another 171 1968 hardtops— a mid-year model featuring roll-down rear windows instead of the original flip-out units— were built with the 425hp "King Kong" V-8.

This impressive scoop, sealed to the Six Pack's large air cleaner by an equally large rubber doughnut, fed cool air directly to those three hungry Holleys. As *Car Life* explained, the scoop "gapes wide open, seemingly ready to ingest all that gets near it including water, dirt, or birds." Although there was no stopping the birds, any water that entered the works was drained away by special drain tubes in the bottom of the air cleaner.

Left
Beneath a 440 Six Pack's oval air cleaner hid these three Holley two-barrel carburetors, totalling 1350cfm, on an Edelbrock aluminum intake manifold. Compression and cam timing for the 390hp 440 Six Pack were the same as the 375hp 440 Magnum with its single Carter four-barrel, but various internal modifications gave the Six Pack version improved high-winding capability. Included were stiff Hemi valve springs, beefed-up rocker arms and connecting rods, and specially machined cam lobes and lifter surfaces to minimize wear due to high valve spring pressures. Maximum Six Pack horsepower came at 4700rpm, compared to 4000rpm for the Magnum 440.

Following page
Although Dodge's exceptionally attractive, restyled 1968 Charger looked sleek, it possessed all the aerodynamics of a brick on NASCAR's superspeedways. Weary of trailing Ford and Mercury on the NASCAR circuit, the Dodge boys placed a group of Charger R/Ts in the hands of Creative Industries in Detroit with the goal being to produce a run of wind-cheating NASCAR homologation models. The result was the Charger 500, an odd concoction marketed as a 1969 model. Up front, a Coronet grille with exposed headlights (all other Chargers had hideaway units) was mounted flush, while in back the tunneled rear window area was filled in and the window mounted flush. The Charger 500 was superior to standard models at high speeds, but aerodynamic responses from Ford made Dodge's first aero warrior obsolete almost before it hit the track

Along with the obvious body modifications, Charger 500s were identified by "500" lettering in the tail's bumblebee stripe and emblems in the grille and below the right taillight. Production of 1969 Charger 500s is estimated at 392 today, even though NASCAR rules specified a homologation minimum of 500 regular production models. Power came from either a 375hp 440 Magnum or the 425hp 426 Hemi. Reportedly, this Hemi-powered Charger 500 is one of sixty-seven known to exist.

Right
Two problems hindered the redesigned 1968 Charger's performance on NASCAR superspeedways: the recessed grille up front served as an anchor as it trapped airflow, while the stylish tunneled rear window area created turbulence, which translated into serious drag. To solve the problem in back, Creative Industries' people fabricated a steel plug to fill in the tunneled backlight, then added a flush-mounted rear window. A similar tactic was applied to the 1969 Daytona and 1970 Superbird.

Ford Motor Company's response to the Charger 500 was the 1969 Talladega and Cyclone Spoiler II, sleek, slippery stockers that forced Dodge designers back to the drawing board. The result was the radical Charger Daytona. Keeping the Charger 500's steel rear window plug, the Daytona also featured a highly aerodynamic steel nose cone and a wild aluminum rear wing. Although the street versions didn't require them, the rear-facing fender scoops needed to clear the oversized tires on racing Daytonas were retained. Dodge built 503 Charger Daytonas in 1969.

Dodge's second aerodynamic NASCAR variant was available to streetside customers with either a 375hp 440 Magnum or 425hp 426 Hemi under the hood. Production was 433 for the 440-equipped Daytonas, and seventy for the Hemi cars. Rarity in the case of this particular Daytona is intensified by its paint scheme. This Bright Seafoam Turquoise Metallic finish, coded Q5, is only known on one other 1969 Daytona.

Right
Like the Charger 500, the Charger Daytona was built by Creative Industries in Detroit. Thanks to its high-flying "towel rack" spoiler and distinctive snout, the Daytona reportedly possessed an excellent 0.29 coefficient of drag. Throw in 426 Hemi power at the track and 200mph was no problem.

Left
Plymouth produced a winged wonder of its own in 1970, applying similar tactics used by the '69 Charger Daytona to its revamped Road Runner body. But while Dodge only had to build 500 Daytonas to make them legal for NASCAR competition, sanctioning officials raised the ante to 1000 in 1970. No problem, Plymouth ended up selling 1,935 Superbirds; 1,084 with the 375hp 440, 716 with the 390hp 440 Six Barrel, and 135 with the 425hp 426 Hemi. After dominating the 1970 NASCAR season, Mopar's winged warriors were banned from competition, transforming the1970 Superbird into a one-year wonder.

Although both Dodge's Daytona and Plymouth's Superbird appeared similar, minor differences in design dominated. Up front, the steel nose cones varied slightly in shape and the Superbird's air inlet—shown here—was located below the tip (Daytona inlets wrapped up slightly to the top side). Both cars used the same fiberglass hideaway headlight buckets, but the Superbird's fender scoops were rounded while the Daytona's were flat on top. In back, the Superbird's wing was taller and swept back further than the Daytona's. Unlike Daytonas, Superbirds also needed vinyl tops to hide required lead work in the rear window area.

The last of Plymouth's GTX models, the 1971 edition, impressed many as a muscle car survivor at a time when factory performance was clearly on the wane. As *Car and Driver's* staff wrote, "we would have to say that the GTX is a step forward on a front where all others are retreating. It is vastly improved over the previous model and only in performance, primarily because of increased weight, has it lost ground." Serious performance buyers could still order the 390hp 440+6 and 425hp Hemi, but a mere 135 chose the tri-carb 440 and only thirty selected the Hemi.

Left
A totally new, bulging body may have helped appearances, but Plymouth's 1971 GTX suffered slightly from the addition of 170 extra pounds and minor detuning of the standard 440 big-block. *Road & Track's* best quarter-mile effort in a 1971 GTX was 14.40sec at 98.7mph showing the 440-powered B-body was still no slouch. This 1971 GTX is one of 2,538 built with the standard 440.

Left
By 1971, increasingly restrictive emissions standards were taking their toll on factory performance as compression ratios started dropping and smog equipment began strangling the last breath out of American muscle cars. Nonetheless, Chrysler stood relatively firm for at least one more year, and Plymouth's veteran 440 Super Commando only lost 5hp in 1971, down to 370 thanks to a compression decrease to 9.7:1.

A retyled, curvaceous body also graced Dodge's 1971 Charger, a Coke-bottle-shaped creation that rolled on a wheelbase two inches shorter than previous editions. Carried over on the new platform was the Charger R/T featuring heavy-duty suspension, various exterior identification including distinctive "door gills" and a blacked-out hood section, and the 370hp 440 Magnum V-8. Also continued into 1971 were the optional 440 Six Pack and 426 Hemi powerplants. Total production of R/T Chargers in 1971 was 3,118.

Loaded with an incredible array of options, including an exceedingly rare power sunroof (only three 1971 Hemi Chargers had this fitted), this Hemi-powered Charger R/T carried a hefty $6,380.60 sticker in 1971. Base price for the Charger R/T was $3,777. Notice the dictation machine at the head of the console. The orange knob below the steering column activates the toothy hood flap.

Right
Surviving for one last year, the famed Hemi received hydraulic valve lifters in 1971, but remained at its intimidating 425hp. Performance for a 1971 Hemi Charger was equally intimidating, registering in the high 13sec range for the quarter-mile. Only sixty-three Hemi Chargers were built for 1971; thirty-three with Torqueflites, thirty with four-speeds.